Bou
Through COVID-19

Overcoming Burnout A Year into the Pandemic

CJ Calvert

Author of Living an Exceptional LIFE

BOUNCING BACK THROUGH COVID-19

Dedicated to the amazing front line workers who have tirelessly served our communities through this challenging year.

To everyone, including the doctors and nurses, teachers and truckers, store clerks and scientists – I extend my heartfelt gratitude.

BOUNCING BACK THROUGH COVID-19

TABLE OF CONTENTS

    Foreword
    Introduction   1

1. **WHAT A YEAR IT'S BEEN**   6
   Pandemic Archetypes, The New Normal,
   Pandemic Fatigue and Mental Health

2. **RESILIENCE**   43
   What Can We Control, The Power of Questions,
   Gratitude

3. **OVERCOMING BURNOUT TO CREATE BALANCE**   78
   Escape is Not Balance, Strategic Breaks, What's
   Missing?

4. **PHYSICAL ENERGY**   130
   Nutrition, Hydration, Sleep, and Fitness

5. **VIRTUAL FATIGUE** 159
   Eye Gaze, Cognitive Load, Reduced Mobility

6. **MANAGING YOUR STRESS MOSQUITOS** 174
   Stop the Event, Manage Your Perspective,
   Change Your Physiology

Conclusion	203
Additional Information & Mental Health Resources	204
Acknowledgments	205
About the Author	206
Endnotes	207

FOREWORD

As a psychiatrist with a traditionally demanding schedule, the first month that COVID-19 broke out my workload was reduced by 50%, as people were simply too afraid to come near the hospital. Since that time however, it has gone back not only to my normal busy 70 to 75 hours per week, but there's now a crushing knock at the door all the time for an additional 15% additional workload that I'm trying to manage and keep at bay. As you can imagine, the ability for some individuals to handle the same experience is different than others. The number one symptom that I hear all my patients talk about whether they have Schizophrenia, Bipolar Disorder, or have never seen a psychiatrist before now, is a lack of motivation, fatigue, feeling "blah", and no energy. The second commonest symptom is anxiety, with the most frequently prescribed medication that I have given through this past year being Lorazepam (Ativan), a benzodiazepine. Certainly my clinical story here resonates exactly with what CJ is talking about in this book.

So as busy as I am these days (and I must admit my workload has gone up at a time when I'm truly trying to cut down), I definitely wanted to take the time to review this book, but as soon as I had entered into the first dozen pages of reading, I found myself truly wanting to read more and turn the next page. *Bouncing Back Through COVID-19* is such a timely book for the experience we are all facing.

CJ illustrates many powerful life skill strategies and overcoming attitudes with his transparent vignettes about what has happened to him and his family member. I would challenge anyone from whatever their walk of life that so long as they can read, they will be inspired by how they can relate to the credibility and lessons that he has depicted from his life's portrait.

I hope my words help to magnetize the heart of a potential reader so they will do themself the great favour of acquiring this book, and even more so to digest every beautiful chapter. This book is not just about overcoming and thriving through COVID-19, but to overcome any adversity in life. CJ Calvert is delivering a well-orchestrated formula of how we can all take this time to reflect on our lives, reset, adjust our course, and improve on a day-to-day basis to meet the goals that we so very much desire to achieve. This book is packed, but not jammed, with very crystal-clear tried-and-true principles for us all to embrace. Hopefully those with the eyes to see and ears to hear will follow both his advice and example. Embracing CJ Calvert's wonderful words around our priorities, balance, attitude, and love of life will lessen the need for any prescription drug, not only during COVID-19, but through any hardship we will endure in our life.

STEPHEN B. STOKL, M.D., F.R.C.P.(C)
Staff Psychiatrist – Southlake Regional Health Centre
Assistant (Adjunct) Professor, Faculty of Medicine,
Dept. of Psychiatry, University of Toronto

Introduction

"We are not all in the same boat. We are all in the same storm. Some are on super-yachts. Some have just the one oar."

— *Damian Barr*

August of 2020, my buddy Andrew went out on the trails with some friends. He was an experienced extreme mountain biker and the weather was perfect for a downhill adventure. Branches and rocks rushed past him in a dizzying blur as he navigated the rough and dangerous trail. To a novice, this would have been a Double Black Diamond run. To him, it was a bunny hill. And then, with one catastrophic mishap, everything crashed into black.

Some time later, his eyes opened. He could see he was in a hospital bed – Sunnybrook Hospital, in Toronto. Tubes and wires protruded from his body as the life support machines whirred dutifully beside him. He noticed his uncle Kevin was by his bedside. After nine days, he was finally emerging from his coma, and his body was wracked with pain. He would later learn he'd suffered multiple brain bleeds, twelve broken ribs, a very damaged diaphragm, a partially crushed esophagus, a torn ear, and severe pulmonary contusions – bruised lungs. Mercifully, he noticed he didn't feel any pain in his legs. Then, it dawned on him that he didn't feel *anything* in his legs.

The doctor's delivered the grim news: Andrew was paralyzed from the mid-chest down. It was their medical opinion that Andrew would not recover feeling from his T7/T8 down, approximately the level of his bottom rib.

Andrew is a young man in the prime of his life. He is not yet married, and just getting started in his career as a financial advisor. This is a tough hand of cards to be dealt to anyone, at any age. Over the next several months, some big decisions would need to be made about his life, including work, housing arrangements, fundraising to buy critical medical equipment, and pursuing alternative stem-cell treatments. But the biggest decision Andrew had to make was the decision to carry on at all.

"There have been some dark days, I'll admit it," Andrew shared over a Zoom with friends and family.

My automatic reaction was to search out and try to share stories with him about other people who have suffered paralysis and led incredible lives – people who accomplished amazing things. People like Rick Hanson, who was paralyzed at 15, went on to become a Paralympian and eventually traveled around the world in his "Man in Motion" tour from 1985-1987. People like W. Mitchell, who was not only paralyzed but suffered burns over his entire body, and went on to become a successful business owner, small-town mayor and a motivational speaker. Mitchell said, "Before my accidents, there were ten thousands things I could do. I could spend the rest of my life dwelling on the things that I had lost, but instead I chose to focus on the nine thousand I still had left."

Andrew is starting to settle into his new life. He is on the lookout for a motorized wheelchair and has already been on a trip to Panama with his uncle to receive the first round of experimental stem-cell treatment for his injury. Andrew tells me, "I have learned in this process how adaptable we as humans are. What one believed to be impossible yesterday, became possible."

Here's the point of sharing this story: if you saw Andrew roll up in his wheelchair to the base of a steep staircase, would you say "Come on man, just start climbing." Of course not – his injury is obvious to your eyes. You would feel compassion, understanding, and empathy for his situation. However, when someone has a mental health issue, do you know what part of the barrier is for them getting support?

The barrier is no one can *see* the injury. You can't really tell by looking at them that someone is depressed. You don't see them sitting in a wheelchair labeled "burned out". And so, when people are suffering from mental health issues, they may not get the support they require.

Additionally, many Canadians don't want to admit out loud if they are suffering. Imagine the stigma associated with sharing this secret with a less-than-supportive boss. *What would they think? Am I lazy? Am I faking this? Am I making excuses to get out of work? Am I an attention-seeker? Am I just being wimpy?*

Thankfully, more and more organizations are doing the good work to promote a healthy work environment that includes support for mental health issues. This is critical, because we are now facing two distinct health emergencies: the virus itself, and the mental health implications of the lockdown and isolation. Both are real and both are serious.

As a professional speaker, I've spent most of the last two decades delivering training to hundreds of world-class organizations on the topics of managing stress, creating balance, and dealing positively with change. But starting in the spring of last year, a new topic request emerged, and became the primary focus of my time:

"How do we navigate through COVID-19?"

Initially the main thrust of my speeches was focused on helping people juggle the logistics of working from home, managing distance learning for the kids, and keeping themselves and their family safe from the virus.

As the months wore on, I started to notice that the world was shifting, and I was noticing the same change in me. After months and months of the pandemic lockdown, of friends and family getting sick from the virus, of juggling all these additional responsibilities, a new focus came to light – we were all getting burned out.

This was predictable for front line heroes like doctors and nurses. But the burnout from the pandemic was as widespread as the virus. It seemed everyone was struggling mentally and emotionally – school teachers, students, truckers, computer programmers – no one was exempt. White-collar knowledge workers, ensconced in the safety of their home and enjoying uninterrupted income, were assumed to be immune to the emotional toil that the pandemic wrought – and yet we (myself included) were just as susceptible as everyone else.

As we reach the one-year mark of the virus shutting down our major cities across the world, it is this new concern that became my focus. **How can people bounce back from the burnout of the pandemic?** After eight months of delivering training on the topic of burnout and resilience through the COVID-19 pandemic, I have attempted here to organize my insights and experiences with you, in the hopes that they would serve you, your family and your organization on your path to wellness.

This book is not an exhaustive clinical account of everything that has happened to us, but rather an unassuming recipe for how we can renew ourselves going forward. Many of the strategies I share may seem familiar, even simplistic – things you probably already know. What I've discovered in life is that many people already retain great wisdom for how to care for themselves; sometimes all we really need is a positive nudge to remind us to follow our own good advice. This entire book is simply a nudge, from one friend to another, to help you get back on track.

With gratitude,
CJ Calvert

Chapter 1: What a Year It's Been

"I thought 2020 would be the year I got everything I wanted. Now I know 2020 is the year I appreciate everything I have."
 - Anonymous

Think back to the beginning of 2020. To me, it seems like a lifetime ago. What were you doing? What was happening in your life? Do you remember your big New Year's Resolution plans that you had laid out, and how you were going to kick off the New Year with a bang? I sure do. I had some fantastic plans and goals ahead of me for 2020 that I was looking forward to accomplishing. And then for me, and probably for you, and the entire world, our plans took a left turn.

Let's walk back through some of what was going on in the news around the world at the start of the year:

- December 31st, 2019. New Year's Eve celebrations around the world mark the end of a decade and the beginning of our "roaring '20s"
- **December 31st, 2019.** The World Health Organization China Country Office is informed of multiple cases of pneumonia from an unknown cause detected in Wuhan City, Hubei Province of China.[i]
- Wildfires in Australia rage uncontrollably. It is estimated that over a billion mammals, birds and reptiles lose their lives in the blaze. The smoke plumes reach New Zealand and can be seen from the International Space Station.
- January 3rd. An American airstrike ordered by President Trump kills Iranian general Qassem Suleimani, potentially sparking a global military conflict
- January 8th. A passenger plane departing Tehran, en route to Kiav, is shot down by Iranian Armed Forces. All 176 aboard are lost, including five Canadians.
- **January 11th.** China reports its first death from the novel coronavirus, after hundreds become ill
- January 18th. Prince Harry renounces his royal title

- January 26th. A helicopter carrying Kobe Bryant and his daughter Gigi, along with seven others, crashes in a hillside northwest of Los Angeles. All aboard are lost
- January 31st. After prolonged BREXIT talks, the United Kingdom officially leaves the European Union
- **February 2nd.** Philippine officials report the first death outside of China linked to the novel coronavirus.
- February 4th. The US news cycle, understandably focused of the upcoming Presidential Election, reports major technical problems in the Iowa caucus. Joe Biden comes in fourth place and faces an uphill battle to secure the Democratic nomination.
- **February 4th.** The Diamond Princess cruise ship, carrying 3,711 passengers, including 237 Canadians, is quarantined off the coast of Japan after the first passenger is diagnosed with COVID-19
- February 5th. President Trump is acquitted in his first impeachment trial
- **February 6th.** Dr. Li Wenliang, the 34-year-old Chinese doctor who had sounded an early warning about the virus outbreak and was reprimanded by Chinese authorities, dies from COVID-19.
- February 9th. The 92nd Academy Awards are held.
- **February 10th.** A team of experts from the World Health Organization, led by Canadian epidemiologist Bruce Aylward, heads to China to study the COVID-19 outbreak
- **February 15th.** The first European death from COVID-19 is reported in France.
- February 18th, the Boy Scouts of America files for bankruptcy

- February 21st. The roads circling the Ontario Legislature are shut down by striking teachers. It is the first time since 1997 that teachers from all major unions stage a simultaneous walkout.
- **February 28th.** The first fatality of COVID-19 on US soil is reported in Seattle. Later, post-mortem tests would show that earlier fatalities in San Francisco occurring on February 6th and 17th were actually due to COVID-19[ii]
- **March 6th.** 100,000 cases of COVID-19 are now reported worldwide.
- **March 7th.** 100 countries now report cases of COVID-19
- **March 9th.** Authorities in BC report the first Canadian death from COVID-19.[iii]
- March 11th. Harvey Weinstein sentenced to 23 years in prison for rape and sexual abuse.
- **March 11th.** The World Health Organization officially recognizes COVID-19 as a pandemic.[iv]
- **March 11th.** The NBA announces it is suspending its season
- **March 11th.** Actor Tom Hanks and Rita Wilson announce they have contracted the coronavirus.
- **March 11th.** President Trump announces that all travel between Europe and the United States is suspended. Panicked American travellers around the world rush to return home.
- **March 12th.** Ontario Premiere Ford tells travelers to go ahead and enjoy their March Break vacations abroad.[v]
- **March 16th.** Prime Minister Trudeau urges all Canadian's travelling abroad should return immediately.[vi]

- **March 18th.** Canada and the United States mutually agree to close their shared border until further notice.
- **March 20th.** Canada reaches 1,000 cases of COVID.[vii]

…. And the virus was just getting started.

We've faced a proverbial tsunami of changes in a very short period of time this last year. Our entire daily experience was upended seemingly overnight. How fast did things change for you? I remember the last two weeks of March in particular. My inbox was flooded with messages from my clients. Rather than reaching out to request my services, they were emailing me to cancel our engagements. Everything was getting cancelled! And since I work on 100% commission as a professional speaker, I watched my income evaporate overnight.

I wasn't alone. Across the nation and around the world, major cities became ghost towns. If you drove through the city streets, you'd be greeted by a scene that looked like it was torn right from a zombie apocalypse movie; there were hardly any cars or people to be found. Businesses ordered their entire staff home. People scurried out of the office towers with banker's boxes and laptops, not sure how long this would last and trying to carry whatever they could in the rush. Small shops turned their open signs over to "closed". Restaurants delivered the brutal news to their wait staff: everything was shut down. The hospitality and restaurant industries were among the hardest hit, as no one was walking through the door.

We started talking about "flattening the curve" and doing our part to slow the spread of the virus. The new media cycle was dominated with daily accounts of how many new cases of the virus had been reported, and the total number of new deaths. Politicians around the world took to the airwaves to offer calm and reassuring leadership; some did not. People scrambled to source and acquire personal protection equipment, and discovered they were now competing on a global scale for the same scarce resources.

What was your experience at home? For us, we were just at the beginning of March break when the "stuff" seemed to really hit the fan. Our son was delighted that mum and dad were both at home to play with and hang out. We were keeping a smile on our faces and doing our best to reassure him, while trading concerned looks with each other. My wife is the HR Director of her organization and was suddenly stepping into the additional role of Pandemic Task Force Leader. Now responsible for ensuring not only the physical safety of her staff and all their tens of thousands of in-person clients, she also had to wade through the voluminous pile of legal and procedural documents that the provincial government was producing each week.[1] It was on her to keep everyone safe, and to her incredible frustration, the rules and regulations seemed to change every week. It felt impossible for her to keep up.

After March break was extended by a week, our Provincial government announced that all in-person classes were officially cancelled for the remainder of the year. Everyone was going online. Teachers scrambled at a moments notice to organize work over Google Classroom and herd the kids together. They deserved a medal for their efforts! Online school was both a blessing and a curse for the kids. Our son's initial reaction was "Woo-hoo!" because it felt like a big vacation: sleeping in, staying up late, playing video games, and

---

[1] With the Infectious Disease Emergency Leave Act and the Reopening Ontario Act.

not enduring any real structure. But soon, he started to miss his routine. A scholar at heart like his Dad, he dearly missed his two favorite classes at school: lunch time and recess. He missed playing with his friends!

Staying inside started to get to all of us. We missed the little things: going to the movies, to restaurants for a family night out, and visiting our friends and family. My family has seven boys born in March and we would traditionally gather together for a big March birthday party. That party was the first event of ours to be cancelled.

What did you end up cancelling or not attending? Birthday parties? Barbeques? School graduations? Sports playoffs? Music Recitals? Weddings? Funerals? Our family has missed out on them all, as I know most everyone else has too.

It wasn't just the "fun" stuff we were missing. A friend of mine from high school, Stacey, passed away unexpectedly from cancer at the young age of 42. It's a funeral I would have attended under any other circumstances.

Has there ever been so many lives lost with so few people able to gather together to attend their funerals? As of March 2021, there have been 2.62 million deaths from COVID. That represents millions of lives that passed that would have ordinarily been celebrated by extended families, friends and loved ones, now with severely restricted attendance. Millions of lives who suffered in the ICU hooked up to respirators, with no capacity for loved ones to be by their bedside; to hold their hand, reminisce about their lives and be there when they passed. Friends of ours, sisters, lost their mom. She went into the hospital with a merely a cough, thinking she'd be out in a few days. A week later she was gone, and the girls couldn't be with their mom.

Our son's childhood babysitter was scheduled to be married this last year; the wedding is now on hold until the pandemic is under control. Another high school friend of mine is engaged and her fiancé is across the border in the States, and they've gone months without being able to see each other. It's caused huge stress for them both with the border being shut down.

We've all tried to adapt to this situation. Families started to celebrate birthdays over Zoom. For some in the Boomer/silver generation, this meant a crash-course on hooking up a webcam for the first time. Thanksgiving for us became a Zoom get-together, as did our March birthday celebration just this last weekend as I finish the book to head to print. Christmas was a tougher one emotionally to shut down, but common sense won the day. We would stand out on the driveway, family would open the door and stand on their porch, and we would chat and give virtual hugs. It was nice to see family over something other than a webcam!

Through it all, society started doing some wacky things. Remember the toilet paper shortage? The craze of people stocking up on essential goods? It was like everyone suddenly had an imaginary bomb shelter in their basement that they needed to prep for a potential nuclear winter. Store shelves ran bare, and businesses had to start to limit the number of items you could buy to offset the mania.

Then there was *Tiger King* on Netflix, featuring Joe Exotic and his cast of associated wing dings. Not really my personal taste, but the popularity of the show was proof positive that people were looking for an escape.

I think it was around April 2020 that I re-watched the movie *Contagion* on Netflix. I promptly decided it best not to share this particular flick with my son. I had seen it in theatres when it came out in 2011 and thought it was an interesting drama. Re-watching it at the onset of the pandemic was one of the most surreal experiences of my life. It was eerie seeing those fictional characters in a movie going through the same motions as the scientists were on our daily news cycle. The same casts of characters were appearing on both my TV screen and my movie screen: the WHO, the CDC – everyone. And to top it off, the whole *Contagion* movie virus was started by a *bat*. In *China*. The screenwriters must have felt a morbid pride in how prescient they were when the real thing exploded around the world.

We also faced an explosion of conspiracy-theory nonsense and disinformation online. Some people believed COVID-19 was a hoax, that it didn't really exist. Some believed in was real, but it was a man-made biological weapon created in a lab funded by Barack Obama, aimed at reducing global population. Anti-maskers would explode in rage at counter staff if they were asked to put on a mask or be forced to leave the restaurant. Family members and friends faced great divisions in their relationships depending on what side of the issues they stood on.

Pandemic Personality Archetypes

As the pandemic spread and lockdowns commenced, we started to see different reactions in people. Some reactions were understandably situation-based; some were personality based. When looking at those initial responses, we can see several generalized styles or archetypes begin to emerge. Many people would see themselves in two or three of these combined. This is not a scientific list; rather, it's a list based on my observations. As you read these, see if you recognize yourself or those around you in any of these archetypes, and if you can think of any other examples.

1. **COVID VACATIONER**. This person was *excited* when the lockdown was announced. Finally, they felt they had time to tackle all those personal-improvement projects they had been putting off. For them, the lockdown felt a little like a "stay-cation." No more commuting to work! Time at home with the family, time to putter in the garden, bake sour bread, go for bike rides and do some online cardio classes.

2. **COVID JUGGLER.** This is the knowledge worker that was able to transition to "work from home." But work from home through COVID was also characterized by doing multiple meetings on Zoom, blurred lines with work/life balance, and filling the role of schoolteacher to kids who were now doing distance learning from the dining room table. The stress of navigating the "new normal" started to wear people down. They were now wearing multiple hats, including caregiving for older family members who needed someone to get them groceries. They were relatively safe, but frazzled.

3. **COVID PRISONER.** This person felt they were under "house arrest" through the lockdown and didn't like it one bit. Their house had become a prison, their freedom taken away from them. They dearly missed human connection – hugging people, being able to socialize, and just get some variety in their day. They were saddened by all the concerts, movies, sports games, restaurants, and social events they couldn't attend. They grieved the loss of holding weddings, graduations and funerals. Some people had

no family or roommates to interact with and faced increased depression through isolation.

4. **COVID WORKER**. This person was the celebrated "essential worker" who braved the dangers of COVID to keep people safe and keep the gears of society turning. They were the doctors and nurses waging war against the virus in hospitals; the personal support workers in long-term care facilities; the counselors helping people through mental health issues. They were the teachers navigating an abrupt change in teaching methods through online learning or trying to keep kids safe in classrooms while the virus raged. They were the farmers, truckers, warehouse workers, delivery drivers and store clerks that kept the shelves filled with food and necessities. They usually faced a greater threat of exposure to the virus and may have struggled with burnout and other mental health issues.

5. **COVID BROKE.** These are the people who faced economic hardship or even financial devastation due to the lockdown. They were the waiters and cooks, the staff working in hotels and travel and airlines who watched their industries be decimated as their business traffic evaporated. They were also the small business owners who had to lay off their staff and close the doors on the business they had built – a heartbreaking experience for any entrepreneur.

6. **COVID SICK.** This is the person who contracted COVID and suffered its effects. Some would feel almost nothing and decide to self-isolate after a positive test results. Some faced the debilitating

effects of the disease as it left them bed-ridden, enduring the worst cold symptoms of their life. Some would be rushed in an ambulance and spend a terrifying week in ICU hooked up to respirators and wonder if this was the end. Some would tragically lose the battle to COVID, not even being able to say goodbye to loved ones. And the victims of COVID were not just those who contracted it, but the family and loved ones around them. This also includes the army of caregivers that worked in the home or in long-term care facilities. Those who tended to a sick family member, fearfully keeping themselves isolated in the home – or tragically losing a family member to the disease.

7. **COVID INNOVATOR**. These were the people who were determined to create something positive out of this global nightmare. They stepped up to 3D print masks, to find personal protection equipment and have it shipped, to retool machines in order to manufacture ventilators. They were also the ones who took the entrepreneurial leap to start a business, whether it was making custom candles, starting an online fitness program, or a food delivery service.

8. **COVID CHEATER**. There were the people who saw the news of government financial support as a way to manipulate the system and line their pockets. With no moral compass, they looked at this as a way to grift the system. Some bought stocks when they had secret knowledge of the impending catastrophe, making sure not to warm others of what they knew. Some bought Lamborghinis. Thankfully this appears to be a small minority of people.

9. **COVID DENIER**. These were the anti-maskers, the science-deniers, and the conspiracy theorists. Some believed that the fear of the virus was overblown; some saw a full-fledge conspiracy by Bill Gates to inject microchips into their body. They would attend public rallies to rage against the system and shout about how their freedoms were being infringed upon. With tragic irony, we would also start to see a few of these same people online as they contracted the disease, explaining how wrong they had been. Some recovered and survived. Some did not.

However you responded through the pandemic, you were impacted. It's one of the very few things in modern human history where an event affected literally everyone directly. Whether you were inspired, devastated, or doing your best to cope, you had to adapt to something you've never faced before.

Navigating the "New" Normal

Living at Work

"Work is interfering with my enjoyment of working from home."
– Anonymous

We are no longer working from home; we are living at work. When looking at the idea of working from home, it's not just the productivity of the employee during "work" hours to consider; it's also the impact on the family member during "home" hours that has also been dramatically affected. Often there is no clear delineation between the two environments for people.

Though people would often decry the morning commute and its impact on their day's schedule, it did offer the benefit of also serving as a clear break for many people between the two major realms in their life. At the end of the workday, people got to leave the office problems behind them, both figuratively and literally, and enjoy the respite of a "chillaxing" night at home. It's true that many employees, even pre-COVID, would reply to an occasional email or work on a spreadsheet after the official workday was done. But people still felt like they were doing it outside the office. Once COVID hit, for knowledge workers, their home became their office.

Also, the vast majority of people did not have a permanent home office prior to the pandemic. At the onset of the first lockdown, people "made do" with whatever room they had. Some plunked down at the kitchen table and it became their home office. Some people held Zoom meetings in their kids bedroom, with posters and stuffed animals offering an odd visual to whatever important meeting they were having, and often a bit of levity. And that was just the room decoration – many people would be conducting serious meetings (or doing television interviews!) and their toddler would wander in at an inopportune time (to the horror of the presenter, and the wry amusement of the viewing participants.)

So the kitchen table starting serving triple duty for many family members as it would be used to eat meals, write financial reports, and finish the kids math homework – simultaneously.

Not only was there no physical boundary between work and home any more, there often became no temporal boundary. Because of the requirements of juggling multiple roles, many family members would have their workday interrupted with home-related stuff; stuff like helping the kids with their schoolwork, making lunches midday for the family and keeping the kids focused rather than playing during school time. Because of the interrupted work schedule, employees would start making up for it by working well past their pre-COVID cutoff time. They'd work until 6pm, or 7pm, or 9pm, until past midnight. And many of their co-workers were doing the same – meaning that a reply you would normally expect within the hour became a reply you'd get once the other employee handled their own personal work/life chaos. The clear lack of a hard cutoff time was as much responsible for people feeling out of balance as the lack of a separate office space.

What many people have found works for them is, where possible, to set up a separate work space inside the home. This might be a guest bedroom that gets designated as the "office". It can also be a corner of a room that you simply say, "that's my work corner."

Also, it helps to decide on a specific cut-off time when work is done for you, and feel completely okay with saying (when it's appropriate for their role) "I'm not looking at another email until tomorrow morning." Some employees make a production of closing the laptop, turning it off and putting it away – right out of sight. Work is now done!

Finally, some employees have created transition rituals for themselves in the morning and at the end of the work day; little practices to give them space and decompress before they shift into the other realm. This can include getting in the car and driving to get a cup of coffee, going for a walk around the block and listening to music, sitting alone at a park (or in the bathtub, or in your living room) and reading a book, or any other unwinding activity.

Leaders Needing to Adjust

"We're being forced into the world's largest work-from-home experiment, and it hasn't been easy." – Saikat Chatterjee

Prior to the pandemic, some managers were decidedly uncomfortable having employees work from home. This stemmed from several factors.

First, our present society grew out of the industrialized revolution where everyone needed to show up at the job site in order to do the job, whether it was standing on an assembly line and adding a widget, typing up reports, or attending meetings. There was no alternative. In the last 30 years, technological advances have created a new class of employee: the knowledge worker. Anyone with a knowledge worker role can, with a laptop and a cellphone, do their job sitting on the beaches of Tahiti while sipping a margarita – or anywhere else in the world you might imagine, as long as you have a reliable internet connection.

The second barrier that people faced was perceived productivity. Leaders worried that staff would "flake off" on the job and get nothing done. After all, you could be watching Netflix while you're logged onto that important meeting... how would the manager know? Prior to the pandemic, you could say you were grinding away while you were actually at the mall shopping.

The third barrier to having people work at home was the leadership ability of their manager. Most managers don't drive results, they drive activity. And the easiest activity to track and manage is "how many minutes is Dave sitting in his seat." The junior manager could glance out his office and confirm that Dave was, in fact, sitting in his seat. Managerial task accomplished. Consider even suggesting the following idea to a new manager: once Dave gets his work done for the day, Dave should be allowed to leave for the rest of the day. The manager would squirm uncomfortably at such a brazen and revolutionary idea. They feel, really deeply and profoundly feel, that Dave just has to be sitting in that chair until 5pm, in order to ensure that work gets done. Why? "Just 'cause."

(By the way, I firmly believe you should manage results, rather than attendance or effort. But that's a topic for another book.)

And then, everyone got sent home.

Overnight, it was no longer a hypothetical issue about how employees would perform at home. Productivity was not the first concern; employee safety was. Many managers were surprised to find that staff actually could get a lot done at home. The potential benefit? Erasing the stressful commute to and from the office, for starters. People weren't dashing out the door in a frenzy to physically arrive on time; they could stroll into their home office in a t-shirt and pyjama pants, enjoying a cup of coffee and starting to glance through emails. The long-term financial benefit to companies could potentially be massive. Imagine how much it costs to maintain the lease payments on huge officer towers, and then imagine dramatically reducing the physical footprint your business requires. If half the staff are working from home, you no longer require the top four floors of the office tower; you can get by with two. Why not?

Last May, Twitter CEO Jack Dorsey announced that going forward all employees would be able to work from home – permanently.[viii] Apple CEO Tim Cook also announced that he felt it unlikely that employees would return to the office before June of 2021.[ix] Bill Gates predicts we will work 30% less days in physical office spaces even after the pandemic.[x] Dozens of other major technology companies have followed suit. In fact, as we march towards vast swaths of society getting vaccinated and we see the eventual retreat of the virus, a new question will be fiercely debated: how much time should employees physically spend in the office?

Distance Learning for Kids

"If you see me talking to myself this week, mind your business. I'm having a parent/teacher conference." – Anonymous

When major cities went into lockdown, most school systems had a choice to make: no learning, or e-learning. With most students having access to reliable Wi-Fi, and school boards in major Canadian cities providing Chromebooks for students, it was the obvious decision to make: all the kids are staying home for the spring of 2020.

The variable in the experience for kids was the support they would receive both from their school system and from their home experience. Not every area has access to the same resources, and not every family has a home environment conducive to learning. Sometimes the best thing in a kid's day is getting away from whatever drama (or trauma) might be occurring at home and escape to the relative structure, normalcy and safety of a brick-and-mortar classroom. And, even with the best of intentions, many good parents had no extra mental or emotional bandwidth to help manage the kids at home while they were juggling their own work pressures as the whole world shut down.

A USA Today article said this of parenting through the pandemic:

"Children can go through divorce, they can go through death, they can go through just an amazing array of things and come out looking pretty good, if they've got somebody who can support them," said Mary Dozier, a psychology professor at the University of Delaware who studies children who have experienced adversity.[xi]

As with employees working from home, the dramatic use of e-learning for students is likely to stay even post-pandemic.[xii] The fact that it can be done is likely to result in a hybrid form of teaching and learning going forward.

But the ability to teach and learn isn't the full school experience. Many kids are grieving the loss of traditional coming-of-age experiences, such as school trips, being involved in clubs, and graduation ceremonies.[xiii] Depending on their age, they are also missing out on the life experiences like physical sports, spending time with friends and dating. All of these socializing activities are important for personal growth and confidence.

Not only that, but the obvious impact of a sedentary lifestyle on kids physical health and mental wellbeing is only magnified during COVID-19.[xiv] It was hard enough pre-COVID to get kids off the video games and outside riding a bike; now the pandemic places an additional barrier. Keeping them inside helps reduce risk of contracting the virus, but it increases mental and physical health issues in kids due to isolation, reduced exercise, and increased "screen time."

Everything is Online

If we thought the world was connected before the pandemic, it's gone to a whole new level this year. Every meeting, every holiday, every connection, seems to be going more and more online. School is online, work is online, friends and family are online, classes are online, watching movies is online, doctor appointments are online, and shopping is online.

Prior to the pandemic, I had never had an Amazon Prime account. Now, I'm a raving fan. In fact, it's become a delightful pleasure to hear the knock at our door and find a little package waiting. It's like Christmas! It sparks a little moment of joy for me. I'm a "book-a-holic"; I buy books faster than I can read them.

Many counselors are doing their work online as it keeps everyone safe. The challenge is that we lose so much communicative energy and information when you're trying to have a conversation over Zoom. It's better than the telephone, because at least you can see people's faces, but creating a focused environment with people in multiple buildings creates its own challenges.

The pandemic has decimated many industries, including the movie industry. Not only are multiplexes shut down, but they are worried they can even financially survive. Warner Brothers announced this year that 2021 would see all new releases being streamed online rather than having an exclusive launch in theatres – and they faced an intense backlash from directors like Christopher Nolan because of it. We saw the movie *Tenet* in theatres twice in the weekend it opened, partly because it was awesome, partly because we wanted to support the theatres sales, but mostly because we didn't know if this would be our only chance to see something live for quite a while. Wonder Woman 1984 came and was gone in a blink because of the lockdown, and we ended up watching it online from home. Disney took movies like *Soul* and the live-action remake of *Mulan* and just skipped right to streaming delivery through their new platform.

Air Travel

The pandemic predictably brought the airline industry to a standstill in April of 2020, grounding approximately 8,500 airplanes, or one third of the world's total commercial passenger fleet.[xv] It's slowly coming back, but to what extend should we expect?

After the 9/11 terrorist attacks, security around air travel immediately and understandably increased. Wait times were dramatically extended. People started to question, both out of fear for personal safety and to save money, whether it made more sense to simply jump on a call rather than jump on a plane. Videoconferencing technology in 2001 certainly existed but was expensive and cumbersome compared to the relative ease we enjoy today. With the ease and inexpense of hosting a Zoom meeting, and near-guaranteed personal safety of their staff, businesses are opting to keep their employees online rather than in the air.

The decrease in flight numbers is not the only change. We already see temperature checks at airports and mandatory quarantines when people enter a country. At the beginning of the pandemic, airlines who wanted passengers to feel safer would leave the middle seat empty. While it makes sense from a safety perspective to do that, it's not economically sustainable. Airlines can't keep their planes in the sky by cutting 1/3 of their sales.[xvi] Either ticket prices go up 50% or people tolerate having a passenger squeezed beside them.

Some airlines such as Air New Zealand are already experimenting with a "digital health certificate" app that proves will provide reassurance to all passengers that the people sitting around them have met the required health standards.[xvii]

With all the challenges facing it, Bill Gates predicts that 50% of air travel will permanently go away.[xviii]

Lockdown & Isolation

The lockdown has been the most dramatic experience, as everyone is in a version of "house arrest". Our neighbors returned from vacation and there were police cars in their driveway – they were to remain in their home for fourteen days or face a major fine. Everyone lamented the shuttering of hair salons and people started developing COVID-19 hairstyles – shaggy and unkempt. Soon after, the braver among us experimented with giving themselves "self-haircuts" at home, and quickly dispatched with repeating the experiment. Zoom camera's went strangely dark for some that week. It's best to leave that stuff to a trained barber.

Shopping at any store became an experience in either lining up around the building, or enjoying curb-side pickup. Stores were quick to layout tape on the ground, showing the distance each shopper should stand away from the next person in line.

Since we enjoy many activities like swimming, rock climbing, laser tag, movies and restaurants, we found ourselves missing those things that had been cancelled.

Emotionally, the biggest challenge for many people was the isolation from others. Isolation is devastating psychologically. If you've got a prisoner facing a thirty-year sentence, what further punishment could you level against them for bad behaviour? You can threaten them with solitary confinement. Human beings don't like isolation; we are social creatures by nature. Because of being cut off from so many of our loved ones, many people took to purchasing pets for the first time, in order than they might have a companion in their home to hold and love and play with.

WHAT A YEAR IT'S BEEN

PANDEMIC FATIGUE AND MENTAL HEALTH

"Some of the most comforting words in the world are 'I am too.' That moment when you find out that your struggle is also someone else's struggle, that you're not alone, and that others have been down the same road." – Anonymous

When the pandemic hit, people weren't sure how long this would drag on. Many people thought we would shut down for a few weeks, and assumed by Easter everything would open right back up. As the weeks marched on, the hope of a swift conclusion to the pandemic started to fade. We all started to think this would drag on longer than originally expected, but we obviously never knew exactly when things would return to normal (and we still don't). There were potential milestones we would muse about aloud. We hoped things will go back to normal when the warm weather came… or the new school year started or Halloween… or Christmas… or when the vaccines got rolled out…or when a miracle occurred… *that's* when things would return to normal. But we couldn't see the end date.

It reminds me of the story of Florence Chadwick, a record-setting long distance swimmer. Born in 1918, she became the youngest person to swim across the San Diego bay at the age of 10. Among her many accomplishments, she swam across the English Channel at the age of 32 in 13 hours and 23 minutes, setting a new world-record. However, on her attempt to cross the 26 miles from Catalina Island to the coast of California, a heavy fog set in. She could no longer see the coastline – the end was no longer in sight. It became too challenging to continue without a clear finish line. Though she had her support team in a small boat beside her, urging her on, she gave up and was pulled out of the water, only to discover that she was just a mile away from the beach. She lost the will to continue because she didn't know how much further she needed to go.[xix] Enduring this pandemic has been a little like that for us. If we knew how much more is required, we could say "It's okay – it's just 87 days left." But without a clear finish line? Our brain gets easily discouraged.

In his book *Transitions*, author William Bridges describes three separate stages of a change: the ending, the neutral zone, and the new beginning.[xx] With most changes in life, there is a clear *ending*; your parent passes away, you move to a new town, you start a new job… we can grieve the loss, accept it and start to come to peace with it being gone. We can also visualize the new reality and adapt to it. However, the experience of this pandemic is very different. Things haven't "ended"; they are in a state of temporary suspended animation. It feels like a permanent "neutral zone." We think they will come back – but aren't 100% sure. We think they will come back by a certain date – but the date keeps shifting. COVID-19 is has a moving "finish line" which keeps us from moving to the next phase of coping or adjusting.

For example, my son and I are big movie buffs. We were both deeply disappointed when theatres closed as we love the summer blockbusters. We are eagerly awaiting the next Marvel superhero movie to come out, but the release date keeps getting pushed back – over… and over… and over. When we hear about a new release date, we now don't really believe it. Without a hard finish line that we can focus on, we feel even more frustration and mental anguish, wondering "how long is this going to go on? Are we going to return to normal? What parts of our life are gone temporarily, and which are gone forever?" It can be exhausting.

When so much of your life feels out of control, it can make you feel better to focus on the little things you *can* control. At the beginning of the pandemic, some people found it motivating to focus on their "I did" lists. Scores of people starting diving into little home-improvement projects. I sure did in our home! I replaced and installed a new dishwasher, installed a new sink in the bathroom, and set up and installed a new Ikea art center/home office desk for my wife. We completely renovated, repainted and refurnished our son's bedroom in the summer, complete with glowing LED lights under the bed and headboard, making it the coolest room in the house. I researched, purchased and assembled all the separate little parts needed for a custom-built home computer – a first for me. Patting myself on the back, I smiled and proudly thought, *Look at what I did today!*

What's the point of an "I did" list? We might have focused on what we had already accomplished each day, rather than how much lay ahead of us. Associate professor of psychology Emily Balcetis, author of *Clearer, Closer, Better: How Successful People See the World*, shares the concept of the "small area hypothesis".[xxi] What this describes is that when we are doing a big task, it's motivating to look at how much we've already done rather than what's left. If you have ten things to do, and you've done two, you focus on the two completed tasks and feel good. If you've done seven, you focus on the three that are left, and you feel good. The smaller amount feels more motivating to focus on.

(An example I have seen is when making a to-do list, some people like to write down things they've accomplished so they can put little check marks and feel good; this becomes an 'I did' list instead, so you feel a sense of progress.)

Think about tackling your garage for spring cleaning. There is so much to overcome you might be de-motivated. Once you get a little section in the corner tidied out, you step back and feel a little swell of pride over what's been done, and it gives you a little boost of energy. You want to have that feeling again, so you decide to tackle the next little pile.

The beginning of the pandemic seemed to bring a flurry of activity, of little projects, little wins, little accomplishments. Each day I could put a pat on my back and say "Good job! Look at the checkmarks I entered on the 'I did' list!" I saw other people diving into their hobbies. My brother made a sourdough culture and became a pastry master. My friends painted positive sayings on rocks and left them in their local park. I enrolled in some music composition courses and wrote some new symphony music for the first time in years. It was a burst of happy activity.

And by August, I found myself sitting on the couch, staring at the wall, all petered out.

What happened?

I started noticing that I was having trouble concentrating. I couldn't keep myself mentally focused on tasks. Each day seemed to slip into the next like a grey mush. I am normally a pretty driven guy, and I found myself languishing in a stupor. I knew this wasn't the real me. I didn't feel necessarily sad, or scared – I just felt drained. I was robotically going through the motions each day.

In her article *Late-Stage Pandemic Is Messing With Your Brain*[xxii], writer Ellen Cushing shares:

> *"We're all walking around with some mild cognitive impairment," said Mike Yassa, a neuroscientist at UC Irvine. "Based on everything we know about the brain, two of the things that are really good for it are physical activity and*

novelty. A thing that's very bad for it is chronic and perpetual stress."

Even though I didn't describe myself as stressed, I would describe myself as being on "high-alert." Every time walking into a store, I would make sure to wear a mask and social distance. Every time a package arrived, I would take it into the bathroom, spray it with Lysol, dump the untouched contents onto the living room carpet, dispose of the box and thoroughly wash my hands. Walking on the sidewalk in the summer, we would leave a wide berth as strangers approached. I was as vigilant as a sentry guard posted in the guard tower of a military base, constantly scanning the tree line for enemy combatants. Staying in this level of hyper vigilance was exhausting. Lisa Butcher, a Vancouver-based Registered Clinical Counsellor says:

"The COVID-19 pandemic has tested our physical and emotional strength as humans, but perhaps most importantly it has forced us to endure an isolation profoundly unfamiliar to us. I think the biggest surprise for me has been the universality of people's feelings. I have had clients from all over the world – South America, Europe, and North America – who all describe the same experiences. As isolating as this pandemic has been, there is a unifying quality to it. Everyone in the world is feeling similar things, which unites us on a global level."

The lockdown was starting to take a toll on me. And it was obvious I wasn't alone – people everywhere were starting to experience some intense emotions. My Dad started to mention that he was bored with being locked inside. He missed going to the gym and to his flying club. My mom, a person who loves hugs, was starved of getting to hug her kids and grandkids. My son missed having friends over for sleepovers. My mother-in-law, alone in her condo, was cut off from friends and family. It was starting to wear on all of us.

In a July 2020 policy paper from CAMH, the mental health crisis caused by the pandemic is concerning. They write:

> *COVID-19 is having a negative impact on Canadians' mental health, with many seeing their stress levels double since the onset of the pandemic. People are struggling with fear and uncertainty about their own health and their loved ones' health, concerns about employment and finances, and the social isolation that comes from public health measures such as quarantining and physical distancing. A recent poll found that 50% of Canadians reported worsening mental health since the pandemic began with many feeling worried (44%) and anxious (41%). One in 10 Canadians polled said that their mental health had worsened 'a lot' as a result of COVID-19. Similar results were found in a survey of Canadian workers, where 81% reported that the pandemic is negatively impacting their mental health, indicating a significant drop in overall worker mental health since the beginning of COVID-19.* [xxiii]

Have you been feeling this way? If you have, I want you to understand you aren't alone. Hundreds of millions of people are feeling this way. We are all going through this strange, globally-shared experience together (which is also very unique.) And we are collectively exhausted from this experience.

We can look back at previous pandemics, like the Spanish Flu of 1918, and get a sense of how people responded in those times to compare our reaction. A more recent comparison is the smaller SARS outbreak in 2003. 8,098 became sick and 774 lives were lost.[xxiv] With the SARS outbreak, we saw some consistent mental health issues crop up; issues that we are predictably seeing again during this pandemic. Those issues include post-traumatic stress disorder, major depressive disorders, and generalized anxiety disorders.[xxv] We are also seeing an increase in domestic abuse[xxvi], self-harm, and tragically, suicide rates.[xxvii]

As we are navigating this new reality, the common symptoms keep cropping up. In their July 2020 article *Emotional Exhaustion during Times of Unrest*, mental health experts at the Mayo clinic say there are a number of symptoms of emotional exhaustion.[xxviii] They list the following symptoms, which are things we should be on the lookout for:

Emotional symptoms include:

- Anxiety
- Apathy
- Depression
- Feeling hopeless
- Feeling powerless or trapped
- Irritability
- Lack of motivation
- Nervousness
- Tearfulness

Physical symptoms include:

- Fatigue
- Headaches
- Lack of appetite
- Sore muscles or muscle tension

Performance symptoms include:

- Failing to meet deadlines
- Lower workplace commitment
- More absences
- Performing work duties more slowly

If you or a loved one are feeling any of these things, there is nothing "bad" about you – your aren't weak, or unintelligent, or fragile, or a failure. You are a normal human being swept up in an abnormal circumstance. It's important not to be harsh or judgmental with yourself. There is little value in giving yourself a "tough love" talk when we're talking about a mental health issue. With exercise, you might say "Hey buddy! Time to get off the couch and hit the weights!" But with emotional exhaustion, a different tactic is required. We need to understand what's going on inside ourselves, how serious it might be, and how to move forward.

What Is The Difference Between Exhaustion, Stress, Burnout And Depression?

We've all had days where we are running on empty. If you're trying to make it through the day on two hours of sleep, you're going to feel **physical exhaustion**. Similarly, you'll feel exhausted if you haven't eaten appropriately, if you are dehydrated, if you've exerted yourself physically for an extended duration (such as intense exercise, running a marathon, or physical labor on a job site) or you've had a long work day without a break. This includes knowledge workers; you don't need to be lifting heavy things to get tired. Merely sitting comfortably at their desk, with no greater exertion than typing on their keyboard will run you down if you don't take a break. Note that you can be in good spirits, have your life going well, and be fully aware that the only thing happening to you is that you simply feel tired. Even if the work is enjoyable and conflict-free, doing fifteen hours non-stop will leave you feeling drained.

Additionally, we all feel **stress** at some point. Since I spend an entire chapter on this later in the book, I will simply say here that stress is our emotional and physiological response to any pressure or danger that we face. Stress is often situation-specific, and you can usually identify exactly what set you off: being cut off in traffic, being late for a meeting, receiving an email that the project has been cancelled, or needing to give a speech in front of a crowd. You can use specific interventions to calm yourself down, such as deep breathing, and within moments feel your stress abate. Because many stressors are often finite (it happens, then it's over) you can bounce back from your stress response pretty quickly using good coping techniques.

We enter the realm of **burnout** when we start describing a chronic and enduring pattern of both physical *and* emotional exhaustion. The term "burnout" was first coined in the 1970s by the American psychologist Herbert Freudenberger.[xxix] Originally he began to see patterns in roles that required caregiving of others, such as doctors and nurses, school teachers and social workers – roles that required some self-sacrifice for the good of others. Over time, researchers building on his work saw that the same patterns of emotional and physical exhaustion would also show up in multiple roles outside of caregiving.

Additional work by Berkley professor Christina Maslach developed a framework for measuring burnout: The Maslach Burnout Inventory.[xxx] They developed five separate "dimensions" for identifying an individual's level of burnout. Those were:

- **Emotional Exhaustion** *("I've got nothing left to give.")*
- **Depersonalization** – loss of feeling towards the people you are serving (clients, patients) *("I no longer care what happens to them.")*
- **Personal Accomplishment** – feelings of professional competence and success at work. *("I am no good at my job.")*
- **Cynicism** – indifference towards one's work *("I don't care about this work anymore.")*
- **Professional Efficacy** – how much you feel your work has a positive and beneficial impact on people. *("What I do doesn't matter.")*

When you face a situation that's been going on for a long time, and you seem to have no ability to change it, you might start feeling powerless. It can affect your attitude towards the problem – you might get pessimistic, cynical, and attempt to protect yourself emotionally by withdrawing your feelings about the situation.

Consider a social worker trying to help inner-city kids in a drug- and crime-infested neighborhood. After getting your hopes up, again and again, that a child will turn themselves around, the crushing pain of watching another life lost to drugs or gang violence will understandably take its toll. Telling yourself "I don't care," might seem like a good defense mechanism, but the problem is deep down you likely *do* care about the situation, and caring about it hurts. You start to disengage from your work. You are no longer passionate, but instead going through the motions robotically. Your motto might shift to "What's the point? It's hopeless," and you can barely muster the energy to get through the day. You are physically exhausted, emotionally numb, and feel like the situation is out of your control.

Burnout is experienced when you face extended, unrelenting stress, often (but not always) due to work-related issues, leaving you emotionally and physically exhausted. This is exactly what we are experiencing through this pandemic. We've watched this scene play out in hospitals around the world this last year, as tear-eyed medical professionals take to YouTube to beg their local leaders for more support, describing the situation they face as a "war zone"[xxxi] or a "horror movie".[xxxii] Many nurses report they've never seen so much life lost in their career. And because of that, as well as the unrelenting schedules, the pressure of inadequate PPE at the onset of the virus, and concern for their own safety – the number of frontline medical professionals seeking out mental health professionals for counseling has skyrocketed.[xxxiii]

But you don't need to be working in a hospital (or even at your job) to face burnout. You could be a caregiver to your 86-year-old parent who lives with you, tending to their needs from 6pm-11pm every night after a day at work. You could be a student studying for your bar exam without a break for days and weeks could face burnout. And, even living and working in the relative safety of your home for the last twelve months can produce burnout – as it has, for countless Canadians.[xxxiv] We've faced the stress of navigating the new normal, juggling new responsibilities with homeschooling kids, keeping ourselves safe, social isolation and the loss of fun activities that would normally reduce stress. All the while, not having control over our situation and not knowing when things will go back to "normal." As Tim Kiladze writes in the *Globe & Mail*, "Why are white collar workers hitting the wall? It's a toxic mix of more work, less fun and some organizational trauma."[xxxv]

Burnout can be predictive of **depression**, and they often have overlapping symptoms, such as fatigue and feeling ineffective in your work. CAMH, The Centre for Addiction and Mental Health, describes clinical depression as:

> *A complex mood disorder caused by various factors, including genetic predisposition, personality, stress and brain chemistry. The main symptom of depression is a sad, despairing mood that is present most days and lasts most of the day, lasts for more than two weeks, and impairs the person's performance at work, at school or in social relationships.*[xxxvi]

Depression can leave you experiencing feelings of guilt or worthlessness, loss of interest in activities you would normally enjoy, and thoughts of self-harm or suicide.

It's critically important that if you or a loved one are suffering from depression, or any other mental health issue, that you immediately reach out for professional support from a doctor or counselor. If your organization has an Employee Assistance Program, their counselors can also help provide the professional support you need.

Some Good News

Whatever you or your loved ones might be facing, it's important to understand that struggling mentally or emotionally during this time is not an indictment against you. If you are stressed, scared, unable to focus or perform at your typically high level, I really encourage you not to be too hard on yourself. Show yourself some grace, compassion, and gentleness. Each of us doing our best to get through this is our own way, and that's okay.

If you are struggling with severe mental health issues, please reach out to a trusted friend or family member, or even better, a doctor or mental health professional. Admitting you need to talk to someone doesn't make you weak, or overreacting, or "crazy". In fact, reaching out to get help is really a sign of strength. We all need help at some point, and only the strong can admit that.

If you are finding, like me, that your brain is foggy and fuzzy, that staying focused is a struggle and you can't remember the simplest things, I have good news for your too. Your brain can bounce back from this because of neuroplasticity – the brains ability to adapt by creating new neural connections. Your brain is remarkably resilient and capable of healing. There are very simple techniques we can use to gently get ourselves back to being the way we were, and I'm going to walk you through them. We are going to get our minds focused, our mood elevated, our bodies recharged, and the solution is simpler than you think.

Let's begin!

Chapter 2: Resilience

"One small crack does not mean that you are broken; it means that you were put to the test and you didn't fall apart."
– Linda Poindexter

We've all met people who seem to have a magical super-power: whatever life throws at them, they manage to keep on keeping-on. They may not even be able to describe how or why, or from where this untapped well of energy springs. They are resilient.

When I ask audiences to define "resilience" in a few words, I typically get the following answers. They describe someone who is:

- positive
- calm
- steadfast
- even-keel
- tenacious
- emotionally intelligent
- cool-headed
- keeps going in tough times

At its heart, resilience is the ability to "bounce back". Whether one is feeling run-down, frazzled, or they've faced legitimate trauma, resilience is the ability to stand up and continue moving forward in the middle of the storm. A resilient person acts like the proverbial rubber band, snapping back into position after being stretched by their circumstances. We need look no further for examples of resilience than the innumerable doctors and nurses waging war against COVID-19 in the emergency rooms across our nation and around the world. Despite the incredible pressure on their time, they face the additional emotional burden of watching so many patients contract COVID-19, and within days in the ICU, pass away. This would take an immense toll on anyone's physical, cognitive and emotional well-being.

Somehow, these incredible men and women get up again and again through this ordeal to selflessly serve their community. Unfortunately, the cost is already weighing heavily on the healthcare industry as the requests for mental health support has skyrocketed during the pandemic. Surely, there must be a strategy one can employ to increase their resilience and have greater adaptive capacity. Fortunately there is, and one key to this strategy lies in the insight gleaned from a terrible time in history.

Man's Search for Meaning

"Although the world is full of suffering, it is also full of the overcoming of it." — Helen Keller

One of the most powerful books I've ever read is *Man's Search for Meaning*, by Dr. Viktor Frankl. This is a somber, emotionally challenging work about one of the darkest times in human history. As an Austrian psychiatrist, Frankl and his family were captured by the Nazi's during WWII and sent to the Auschwitz concentration camp. Watching his loved one's lives extinguished before him, Frankl found that he somehow was spared from the gas chambers.

He was soon struck by a vision: it was of himself, standing on a stage, addressing an audience of attentive listeners. In his vision, he was showered, clean-shaven, and wearing a freshly pressed suit, shirt and tie. He was lecturing the audience, sharing the story of the terrible circumstances of the concentration camp. He was doing this for one reason:

to ensure that people were aware of these events, that they may never again occur.

This vision was so compelling to Frankl that he was filled with a determination to survive. He must survive, he told himself, in order to make this vision come true and share this story. The importance of sharing his message transcended his personal suffering at the moment. In fact, it became his driving reason for being. He found, in the darkness and horrors of the concentration camp, a tiny beacon of light that helped pull him through each day: he had found a reason to continue living.

As Nietzsche said, "He who has a 'why' to live for can bear almost any 'how'." This initial revelation for Frankl was nurtured and eventually blossomed into an entire field of therapy that he pioneered, called logotherapy. Logotherapy states that life has meaning and purpose, and the pursuit of that greater purpose can offset and help treat depression.[xxxvii]

Through the daily horrors that he faced, he began to see that some prisoners were more adept at survival than others. Being a psychiatrist, and having little else but his personal suffering to experience, he turned his attention towards these extraordinary fellow prisoners in an attempt to understand what he was witnessing and personally experiencing.

He realized that the German's could do anything they wanted to do to his *body*; they could deny him food, sleep and comfort. They could work him till he collapsed in exhaustion or fell over dead. They could take away his dignity. They could humiliate him, strike him, torture him – even execute him. But they couldn't make him *think* or *feel* a certain way. This insight was a revelation to Frankl. He wrote:

"We who lived in concentration camps can remember the men who walked through the huts comforting others, giving away their last piece of bread. They may have been few in

number, but they offer sufficient proof that everything can be taken from a man but one thing: the last of the human freedoms – to choose one's attitude in any given set of circumstances, to choose one's own way."[xxxviii]

Frankl's insight was so powerful, and remains true throughout all of human history. It is made clearer by the comparative horror of his situation, and allows us to see that whatever we are personally facing, we can still apply his wisdom. Whatever is happening external to us, we can always choose the way we think about it.

What CAN We Control?

"No matter how bleak or menacing a situation may appear, it does not entirely own us. It can't take away our freedom to respond, our power to take action." — Ryder Carroll

It is psychologically debilitating to feel that you have no control over the situation you are in; to feel that you are powerless, without influence, without a voice or agency over the scenario you face.

Stephen Covey, author of *7 Habits of Highly Effective People*, describes the Circle of Concern and the Circle of Influence[xxxix]. There are many things in life that "concern" us – things that we actually care about. This, by extension, means there are some things that we do *not* care about. For example, you may not care if there is a storm happening over Jupiter. But you probably care if there is a storm happening directly over your home. It is inside your **circle of concern.**

However, you cannot control or influence a storm over your house.

This brings us to the second circle, smaller and inside the first circle. This second circle is the **circle of control**. There are some things you have total or massive control over, and some things you can only partially control or influence. For example, you have a lot of control over your finances, but not total control. You cannot control the world economy, national interest rates, the stock market, the actions of your business customers or competitors, or if your boss has money in the budget to give you a raise.

However, two people with the same salary can start their career at 25, end it at 65, and be in a completely different financial position. Why? Because there are things we can control. One guy might save every penny, and the other guy blows all his money on nonsense and wracks up a huge credit card debt. Each of us *can* control if we write out a personal budget, save money judiciously, avoid purchasing things on credit, invest wisely, increase the value we offer in our career through increasing our skills, working harder, and earning additional income through things like rental properties, stock investments or online businesses. There is a lot you *can* control.

When faced with a situation like the COVID-19 pandemic, there is a lot that is out of our control. It's normal to feel overwhelmed and powerless. We can't control many things, including:

- The global spread of the virus
- The manufacturing of the various vaccines
- The distribution of the vaccines
- Other people's behavior, including whether they wear a mask, social distance and wash their hands

- Other people reading and believing conspiracy theories online
- Whether people take the vaccine
- The impact of rolling shutdowns on the economy
- The psychological impact of isolation on society
- The impact of school shutdowns on other families
- Depending on our role, whether our personal workplace and job allows us to work safely from home
- Whether our company survives the storm financially

We have almost zero control over these things, especially on a global scale.

So, what *can* we control in a situation like this?

There is one thing that we can always control. It's something that everyone can control in every situation, whether they believe it or not, agree with it or not, or are good at it or not. We can control the **way we respond**.

Don't believe me? Well then, here's an important (really, a life-changing) question for you to consider: Is it possible to take two people, put them in the identical situation, have the exact same thing happen to them, and yet **have them respond in completely different ways?** Meaning, is it possible to have one person remain completely calm, and have the other person fly off the handle in a whirlwind of rage, tears, or self-destructive behavior?

The answer is an absolute YES.

You've probably been in multiple scenarios where you watched someone have a meltdown over something you thought was ridiculous. Similarly, you've probably had moments where you were really upset, and the people around you simply shrugged it off.

Why the difference in our reactions? This is a really, *really* important idea to understand. If you can grasp this, your *whole life* is going to change – instantly, profoundly, and forever.

Stuck in the Elevator

Imagine this scenario: three people are trapped in an elevator. One person is incredibly frustrated and angry at the inconvenience to their day. The second person is cracking jokes, imagining that they might pull a "Mission: Impossible" and climb out of the escape hatch in the roof. The third person suffers from claustrophobia, and is trembling with fear.

Here is my trick question for you to consider: did the elevator *make* the claustrophobic feel fear? Did it trigger an emotional response?

Consider any scientist when they approach solving a problem. They are going to want to isolate each variable in the process and test that variable. So, let's isolate the variables and identify what is constant in the equation. You have three people in the same elevator, all in the identical scenario (being stuck), and experiencing three wildly different cognitive, emotional and physiological responses. What is the constant in this equation? The *situation* is the constant. The elevator being stuck, and the people all stuck inside it, is exactly the same for all three of them.

Now, consider: what are the variables in the equation that would produce such wildly different responses. Have you figured it out?

The *people* are the variable in the equation.

That's right: we are the variable. And specifically, the way each of us *thinks* is the variable. Meaning, the internal story we tell ourselves about the situation we are in (our explanatory style[xl]) is what is primarily influencing our reaction to the situation – not the situation itself.

Let's go back to the three people in the elevator. What story was the first person telling themselves? Probably "This is awful and unjust and I am going to make someone pay!" What was the second person saying? "This is a tad inconvenient and mildly amusing." What was the story the claustrophobic person was telling themself? Probably something like: "I am in danger. The walls are closing in on me. I can't breathe. I am going to be trapped here forever. The cable will snap. We will plummet to the ground. I am going to DIE IN HERE."

You can bet that any one of us – myself included – who legitimately believed they were going to die would react the same way they did. So, to conclude this line of thought: was being inside the elevator making the claustrophobic upset, or was their story about the elevator making them upset?

Their *story* was. And friends, we have the power to change the story we tell ourselves. It may not be easy to do. It may take a lot of work, and a lot of conscious re-scripting of our worldview, belief systems, and internal dialogue. You may have faced legitimate experiential trauma – trauma that has left a profound mark on the way you see people and situations. But with work and practice, you can take back control of your story.

What Shapes our Story?

"Nothing is either good or bad, but thinking makes it so" –
William Shakespeare

Invariably, I will have some people disagree with me when I suggest that their internal dialogue is responsible for a lot of their emotional angst. "Surely, this can't be true!" As a parent of a now 13-year-old son, there were a few times when he was younger that he blurted out the phrase, "But Dad! That other kid *made* me mad!" No; no he didn't.

Our story is shaped by all of our life experiences; everything we ever saw, experienced, felt, heard, read, learned, and thought. It was shaped by the books we read, how our parents behaved, their worldview and belief systems, every tragic shred of mistreatment we endured, every injustice, every broken promise, every perceived insult or disrespect, our teachers and their behavior, how the other kids in school treated us, trauma we faced and the meaning we attached to those events, everything we see on the news and see on social media. ALL of that shapes our worldview.

Consider the typical audience in a comedy club when the comedian cracks a joke. Ninety-nine people laugh, and 1 person feels offended and angry at the joke. Is this possible? You bet. Why? I'm willing to bet that the person who is hurt and offended by the joke has had different life experiences than the rest. Perhaps they've faced horrific injustice, and that injustice has changed the way they think. We all feel angry when our value system is violated. But one person's value system might be very different from another's, which means different things will offend and upset each of us.

We sometimes assume, often incorrectly, that people are supposed to share our value system – which they ought to uphold and cherish the things we do, and feel offended by the things we do. We assume, often incorrectly, that our way of looking at the world must be the right way.

Consider the 9/11 terrorist attacks. My experience that Tuesday morning is burned into my memory forever, as I am sure it is for you as well. I was at my sales office when we started getting word that something big had happened in New York City. We switched the televisions on and watched in horror as the heart-wrenching events of that morning unfolded. I felt every awful emotion one could feel: grief, anger, sadness, and terror. Why? Because those events violated my value system. My value system says, "murdering thousands of innocent people is horrifyingly evil."

On the other side of the planet, the Al Qaeda were watching the same news footage as we were, but they had a very different emotional reaction. Their reaction was celebratory. They were delighted to watch the carnage unfold. Why was this their emotional reaction? Because, as insane as this may seem to us, their value system said, "we are simply accomplishing our mission."

Now consider one example the experience of COVID-19 and our emotions surrounding it. I've watched in disgust the online videos of anti-maskers in retail stores openly harassing and, in some circumstances, violently beating the store clerks, because the store clerk asked them to wear a mask. Why would this illicit a violent reaction from some people? Because those people told themselves a story that being forced to wear a mask was such a moral offense that the only proper response was physical violence. That story was based on their worldview.

My point is this: people's personal story, shaped by their value system, creates their emotional response to a situation – just like ours does to us.

Can Anything Else Affect Your Emotions?

There is one additional variable that can shift your emotional state in any given moment: your current brain chemistry. It is very unlikely that your worldview and way of thinking will change from Monday to Friday (short of experiencing a life-altering event.) But your brain chemistry? That can change between 8:00 am and 8:01. Make a measurable and dramatic change in your brain chemistry and you are guaranteed to exacerbate your stress response to stimuli that would normally illicit a mere shrug. Meaning, something that may not bug you on Monday might end up really bugging you on Friday, and it has nothing to do with your value system or life experience. In this case, it's probably brain chemistry. So, what are the usual suspects that might affect your brain chemistry? Here are a few things to be on the lookout for:

- **Fatigue**. If you an exhausted, running on just 90 minutes of sleep, having been up all night working or tending to a sick family member, you might find that little things which typically wouldn't phase you can really tick you off.[xli]

- **Hunger**. If your blood sugar is plummeting because you haven't eaten for hours, you may find the accompanying hunger-headache comes with a dose of irritability.[xlii]
- **Pain**. If you've got a broken toe, a broken back, a splitting migraine headache, or any other pain-inducing ailment, you'll more easily lose your cool.[xliii]
- **A physical change**. If you are pregnant, going through menopause, or experiencing a change in hormone levels due to underlying physical conditions, this may affect your emotional state.
- **Unabsorbed adrenaline**. If you just received a phone call that a family member was in a serious accident, you are flooded with adrenaline and cortisol. It's going to take some time for those chemicals to dissipate and be re-absorbed. During that time, smaller irritants will seem magnified to you because you are already wound up.[xliv]

It's generally a good idea, when you can feel that you are getting emotionally overwhelmed or spiraling down a negative path, to pause and check in with yourself. Ask yourself, "Am I physically feeling good today? How was I feeling moments before this trigger occurred?" Hopefully we are each self-aware enough to admit to ourselves when we've gotten up on the wrong side of the bed, and can intuitively sense we are already grumpy and overreacting to the situation before us. So, the next time we start snapping, perhaps we ought to run down a quick internal checklist: am I tired, hungry, in pain, or already upset about something unrelated? If we are, it's best to mention this diplomatically and apologetically to anyone with the misfortune of being in the blast radius of our poor reaction. A courtesy, "I'm really sorry – I'm not in a good place today. You've done nothing wrong," goes a long way toward maintain the good graces of your colleagues and loved ones.

The Worst Day of My Life

"You never know how strong you are, until being strong is your only choice." – Bob Marley

You might be thinking, "surely this idea of managing my story only applies to the small stuff… right? Comedy clubs and being stuck in an elevator? Having the photocopier jam or being caught in traffic? Surely this can't apply to the really big things in life – the truly traumatic events?

Yes; it still absolutely applies.

On Friday, December 7th, 2018, our son Braydon was in the gym after school. He and his friends were playing on a large crash mat. In one fateful moment, our son overshot the crash mat and smashed his skull onto the hard gym floor. Tears flowed, a big goose-egg bump appeared, ice was applied, and parents were called. My wife and I both rushed to get to him.

We were quite concerned that he had a concussion, and discussed bringing him to the hospital immediately. However, having spent many days and nights sitting for hours in discomfort in the hospital waiting room, only to be given a cursory examination and then being sent home, we decided instead that we would get him home, get him comfortable, and closely monitor his situation. If anything changed, we'd race to emerg.

We noticed as the night progressed that he was uncharacteristically lethargic. My wife (who is brilliant) took it upon herself to ask him, every hour, to repeat his personal information: his name, address, birthdate, etc. He would answer. She would wake him up each hour and ask, and he would grudgingly comply.

At 2 am I heard him weeping in his bed complaining that he was in terrible pain; he said it felt like his head was splitting open. We decided after phoning Telehealth that it was time to take him to the hospital.

At 5 am in the waiting room of the hospital, my wife asked Braydon, "Hey buddy, what's your name?" My son didn't respond. He no longer knew that his name was Braydon, he no longer recognized his mom, and he started muttering nonsensical gibberish. He started vomiting. He started seizing.

What we didn't realize was that he had suffered a traumatic brain injury, and blood had been pooling inside the front of his skull for 12 hours, creating increasing pressure against his prefrontal cortex. He was placed on anti-seizure medication and put in restraints. An ORNGE trauma helicopter was called to airlift him to Sick Kids hospital, downtown Toronto. With too much fog to take off, the chopper was grounded, and we had to wait agonizingly for a ground trauma ambulance to arrive.

My wife turned to the surgeon and asked, "Is he going to be okay?"

To which the surgeon replied, "We are going to do everything we can." We've both watched enough television ER shows to know that this was a terrible answer. My wife looked at me with tear-filled eyes and said, "He could die from this."

She rode in the trauma ambulance with me following in the car behind. Later she would tell me that she asked the trauma nurse, "Is this fatal?" To which the trauma nurse replied, "We're going to get him to Sick Kids Hospital and give him the best care we can."

The next 48 hours were an emotional blur fueled by adrenaline, caffeine and grief. Our son was in the PICU in a medically-induced coma on life support with wires and tubes flowing out of him. We didn't honestly know if he would live through the night. Family members flew in to see him. Others called to say over the phone they loved him in case it was their last chance to do so. Through this ordeal, we couldn't do anything but sit by his bedside and wait.

I found myself writing out all of the possible outcomes as I saw them. They included:

- He could die
- He could be in a coma forever
- He could wake up but be in a wheelchair and disabled forever
- He could wake up, be able to walk and talk and feed and bath himself, but have severe emotional and cognitive issues
- He could wake up and have minor emotional and cognitive issues
- He could wake up and be fine

I resolved, sitting by his hospital bed, that if he could just wake up, so that I could hug him and tell him that I was his Dad and I loved him, and have him recognize me – I could deal with everything else.

Mercifully, on Sunday the brain bleeding stopped. He slowly came out of the coma. When he could speak and was more alert, the doctors started testing him cognitively. They asked him to name every animal he could think of in sixty seconds. He could only remember three. We despaired what his future would hold for him.

After a few days, we got everything arranged for him to be discharged and transferred to a wonderful clinic in Toronto, the Holland Bloorview Kids Rehabilitation Hospital. We lived there until January 31st. Our son began an aggressive rehabilitation schedule, needing to relearn how to properly read, write, walk – you name it.

This whole experience was the worst thing we had each gone through. My wife was truly the rock that held the family together. She was not only the driving force guiding his therapy, never leaving his side; she was simultaneously enduring some pretty significant challenges in her work.

Here is my whole point to telling the story. During this experience, a family member asked me "Why don't you have Post Traumatic Stress Disorder? Why haven't you been prescribed anti-depressants? Why aren't you needing to see a counselor?"

You see, among other factors, I was telling myself a story. A very specific, intentional story. And it would be understandable for most anyone to tell themselves another story. The story many people facing a similar scenario might tell themselves repeatedly is "He almost died. He almost died. He almost died." And it would be understandable to play that story in a loop, over and over in your head, reliving every image and emotion and feeling horrified and traumatized with every replay of the video in your brain.

Instead, the story I told myself was, "Thank goodness he lived."

Thank goodness he lived! All I could see – really, all I was *willing* to see - was that he was walking and talking. He could feed himself, dress himself, use the bathroom, play games, laugh, and tell stories. He would one day be able to finish school, get a job, get married and start a family. He was alive. By most outward appearances, he basically looked and acted like a normal kid. That's what I had prayed for. That's what I wished above all else would happen, and miraculously, that's what happened.

I could choose to focus on what was wrong in the situation, or I could choose to see what was right. Regardless of the situation, we *always* get a choice.

To end the story on a lighter note, the day we were discharged from Holland Bloorview, we had a team of ten doctors, therapists, and neurosurgeons all sitting around a conference table with us, and his teacher on the phone. The doctors informed Braydon that because of his injury, his cognitive processing speed had dropped to the 5th percentile. Not good, right?

Then the doctors said, "Now Braydon: to improve your processing speed, we really recommend you play a LOT of video games."

His eyes opened wide and he looked at me with a big grin.

"You hear that Dad?" he laughed. "My homework is to play a lot of videogames! Woo-hoo!"

You have never seen a more delighted 11-year-old.

How Do We Change Our Story?

"My barn having burned down, I can now see the moon." –
Mizuta Masahide

The first step towards changing your story is **acknowledging your current story**. Since it's often subconscious and produced in the blink of an eye, the way you can elicit your subconscious story is to ask yourself out loud what is happening in this situation, what is the cause and result of this situation, and what it means to you.

Here's a simple example, and a common experience for most people. Imagine you are driving down the road and you see a car approaching quickly in the rear-view mirror. It is weaving around cars and it zips right past you. Why do you suppose the car is driving fast? Answer below:

"The reason the car is driving fast is because _____

_____

Now, I'll admit to a personal pet-peeve. I tend to get pretty annoyed with cars that are speeding. Why? Because when I ask my brain why the car might be going fast, here's the answer my brain generates:

"The reason the car is going fast is because the driver is a thoughtless teenage punk who doesn't care about the safety of other drivers. In fact, he's likely to injure or kill someone!"

So, if that's my story, what sort of emotional response do you suppose that story evokes? You guessed it: anger. In fact, whenever anyone violates your value system, you're going to get angry. Since my value system includes "driving in a way that doesn't wipe out a minivan full of kids", I'm going to get angry.

Now, imagine this variation on the story: picture the car weaving through traffic and it starts to pass you. You've already passed judgment on the driver, and you feel the anger starting to well up. Just as the car passes you, you can now see inside the car and see what's happening.

My friend, is there ever a reason why a car might be driving really quickly on the road, and not only would we not be angry, we would actually feel concern or compassion towards the driver? Think about your answer:

_____

You guessed it: if there is a medical emergency.

If you can look inside the car and see that it's someone being rushed to the hospital – whether it's a lady giving birth, a man having a heart attack, or a kid with blood all over them – you wouldn't feel anger. Your anger would evaporate as quickly as flipping a light switch. And you'd probably feel a little embarrassed by your reaction.

The problem we face through our lives is that we don't often get to see inside the car. It just zips on by, disappearing into the distance. And now we are left with a CHOICE: We can choose to invent an ugly story to explain what's happened, or we can choose to invent a forgiving story to explain what's happened. You don't get to choose your emotions directly. You get to choose the story you tell yourself about your situation, and your story generates your emotions.

Which story do you choose? An ugly story, or a forgiving story? You can choose to say, "It's a thoughtless jerk!" And that ugly story will produce an ugly emotion. Or, you could choose to say, "Maybe they are rushing to the hospital; I hope everything's okay." And that story will produce a compassionate emotion. It's your choice.

A few years ago, our son had a new playmate move into our neighborhood. As kids do, they eventually had each other over for play-dates and sleepovers, and my wife exchanged numbers with the other parent to arrange the details. Well, once my wife's phone number was shared, the other little boy got a hold of it, and started calling my wife at work. All. The. Time. It got to the point where my wife was getting really frustrated with this – she was getting calls all through the day, asking:

"Are you still at the office?"

"Have you left work yet?"

"When are you going to arrive home?"

It was clear to my wife that this little boy was obviously selfish, he was obviously giving no thought to how he was interrupting her busy day, and he was obviously just prodding my wife to get home sooner so that our son was free to come out and play.

This went on for a while, and finally my wife commented to our son that this behavior was getting out of hand – the other kid needed to stop calling all the time. Our son listened intently, and being the gentle soul, agreed the calling needed to stop.

"I'll let him know to stop calling mom," Braydon said. Then he thought about it and said, "I guess the reason he is calling is because his mom died last year, and you remind him a little of his mom. And he wants to make sure you arrive home safely."

Well, you could have knocked my wife over with a feather. With a big lump in her throat, she said quietly, "No, it's okay. He can keep calling me."

When something is happening around you, pay attention to the story you are telling yourself. You might find that a different story can help you handle things better.

Ask Yourself Positive Questions

Our brain tends to notice what we ask it to notice. Look around the room you are sitting in right now. I challenge you to take note of everything red – I can see a red book, a red binder, a red pen, a red icon on my computer screen… I can see over a dozen red things on first glance.

Okay, all finished? Now, focusing your eyes just on this book page, I want you to name out loud everything you saw that was…. blue.

Didn't see that coming? Well, now your brain is scrambling, because it wasn't looking for blue before.

In our brains we have a file folder called a Reticular Activating System, or RAS. Your RAS helps you notice whatever you've decided is significant to notice. Anything new tends to get noticed, because we are looking out for threats. So, if someone hangs a new picture on the wall, you'll notice it. However, leave it there long enough, and you'll stop noticing it because it's no longer novel. If something has personal or emotional significance, you'll notice it right away. For example, a friend of mine starting working at a charity that I'd never heard of. Once they were employed there, I noticed the signs of that charity all over town.

Here's another example. What type of car do you drive? If you're anything like me, the first week you got your car, you started to notice something really strange: there were a hundred of the exact same make and model as your car on the road all around you. In fact, you probably still notice your car model today when people drive by you.

What's the point? If you ask your brain to notice something red, it will notice something red. If you ask your brain to notice a Mazda, you'll notice a Mazda.

If you ask your brain to notice something *good* in your situation, it will notice something good in your situation.

The fastest way to shift your story is to ask yourself positive questions. This is different from making a positive statement, or using a positive affirmation. If things seem really crummy in your life, and you say out loud "Things are just dandy!" you are likely to shake your head and disagree with yourself as you say it. You can feel the statement is disingenuous.

However, asking a question forces your brain to look for an answer. Whatever question you ask, your brain will go after the answer like a heat-seeking missile. If you ask a negative question, you will tend to get a negative answer. If you ask a positive question, you will tend to get a positive answer.

For example: if I ask you to name everything wrong with your house, or your boss, or your family, I'm sure you can come up with examples. Notice how quickly your mind shifts to the negative when you ask negative questions; your house looks run-down. Ask instead, "What's great about my house? What's great about my spouse? What's great about my job?" And you will come up with positive answers.

Consider the following statements and the examples provided, and create your own responses.

Situation:	"I am stuck working at home during the pandemic."
What's Great:	_____
Situation:	"I have to wait six months before I can get the vaccine."
What's Great:	_____
Situation:	"Being cooped up in my house with my spouse and kids is driving me crazy."
What's Great:	_____

If you are stuck at home working during the pandemic, what is great is that you still have a job. There are countless millions of people who have faced reduced hours, layoffs, business closure, and financial devastation during COVID. If you have the privilege of still being employed, I guarantee you there are ten million people who would happily trade places with you in an instant. There are people standing in breadlines in the US who, a year ago, would never have imagined their financial situation would have devolved to this.

If you are frustrated that you have to wait six months for your vaccine shot, what is amazing is that there is even a vaccine in existence that you can receive. In fact, there are several, all with extremely high rates of efficacy and low rates of severe allergic reaction. It is near-miraculous that labs around the world were able to marshal their talent, energy and resources to solve this problem in record-time. There was no guarantee that their solution to creating the vaccine would work. Without their successful efforts, we would still be wondering when a vaccine would arrive at all.

Feeling cooped up in your home with your family? Perhaps instead it would be helpful to step back and give thanks that you have a family, that you have people you can safely interact with. It's a whole other world of psychological hurt to go through this pandemic alone in your apartment. Rather than feel frustrated, put this book down and go wrap your arms around your family and tell them how much you love them and are thankful you can be there for each other during the pandemic.

Interestingly, you can actually change the physical structure of your brain, and change it to become more positive – or any other attribute. How? Hebb's Rule, theorized by Donald Hebb in his book *The Organization of Behavior*,[xlv] attempts to explain neuroplasticity. This theory has been simplified into the popular statement "brain cells that fire together, wire together." In layman's terms, the more times you intensely repeat a thought pattern or behavior pattern, the stronger the connection between your brain cells becomes. So the next time you want to repeat that same thought pattern or behaviour, it becomes more automatic and easier to initiate. This can have negative effects, such as a person who is quick to anger is more likely to lash out in anger, and it can have positive effects – such as a person who consistently thinks positive thoughts is more likely to automatically think those thoughts.

The more times you think a thought, the more automatic that thought pattern becomes. So get in the habit of being positive!

Focus on Self-Efficacy - What Are You PROUD Of?

"When we long for life without difficulties, remind us that oaks grow strong in contrary winds and diamonds are made under pressure." – Peter Marshall

One way to increase resilience is to increase your perception of what you can control. Your personal belief on how successful you can be at handling a tough situation is referred to by psychologists as "self-efficacy." If you've got high levels of self-efficacy, you've got a higher level of resilience to new stressors. [xlvi]

So how can you increase your self-efficacy? One great way of doing this is to recall moments in your life where you overcame a problem or accomplished a difficult task. Tony Robbins even coined a phrase for this: Victorious References. You want to create a list of everything powerful and positive you've done… every challenge you've overcome… every victory you have enjoyed. Focusing on these things is very powerful. Not only does it change your mind set in the moment, but by polishing up your memories and having this list mentally ready at a moment's notice, the next time you face a really tough situation, you can literally say to yourself, "Hey – I've survived worse. I've handled bigger problems that this before."

Take a moment and write down the ten biggest victories of your life, where you had to push yourself to take action and prevail. This could be accomplishing a hard-earned goal like getting your PhD, escaping some negative life circumstances, overcoming addiction, reaching a level of professional success, solving a problem, or managing your fear of public speaking and doing a great presentation.

My Top 10 Victories Are:

_____
_____
_____
_____
_____
_____
_____
_____
_____
_____

The Power of Gratitude

"Do not spoil what you have by desiring what you have not; remember that what you now have was once among the things you only hoped for." – Epicurus

For some reason, it seems easier for most people to focus on what isn't working well in their lives. We are so focused on what we don't have, compared to the next guy, but as soon as we get what we want, we complain about why it isn't perfect! If you are taking the bus, all you complain about is that you don't have a car. As soon as you have a car, you notice it doesn't have power windows. When you've got power windows, you notice that you don't have a Blue Ray player and 60" curved television screen. When you get that, you notice that you don't have a new Playstation 5 for the kids. It's absolutely amazing how we complain about what we don't have!

One of the greatest gifts you can give yourself is the quiet pause of reflection; simply stopping to consider every blessing that you enjoy in your life. When times seem troubling, it helps to consider everything good for which we have to be thankful. We are never more aware of how lucky we are to be able to walk, than when we see another unfortunate soul in a wheelchair beside us. And yet, the person in the wheelchair, with the proper mental attitude, may have a more rewarding life than ours simply because they choose to focus on the fact that they can still see the sunset, hear a symphony or the words "I love you", taste chocolate, hold the hand of their loved ones and smell the roses along life's journey.

Using gratitude as a tool for managing our emotions is a very popular coping mechanism in a hospital when someone faces a serious injury. Rather than focus on the injury, the person can look to the bed beside them and say "I may have lost my hand in the car accident, but the guy beside me has become paralyzed. I'm so lucky to be alive."

I keep a newspaper article in my office, scotch-taped to the wall. It's a story of a farmer from Ontario, who several years ago lost his seven children, and his wife who was pregnant with their eighth child, in a fire that eradicated his home and his family in one night. The photo is of the farmer holding the white casket of his little 18-month old baby in his arms and placing her in the ground. This isn't a happy picture, and it doesn't lift me up; rather, it offers perspective.

You see, any day I come home and I feel like I've had a "tough day" and I feel a little down, I need only look at that photograph and the tragedy that this poor man faced and realize how incredibly blessed that I am. I have absolutely ZERO real problems in my life.

It can be easy to get swept up in the challenges we face, particularly through this year of the pandemic. Imagine for a moment that you were living in a third-world country in a hut with a corrugated metal roof, and COVID-19 came roaring through your village. You have no hospital, no reliable infrastructure or utilities, no clean drinking water, no heat, no predictable food source – nothing. Imagine there isn't even a functioning government. Imagine you face local warlords and their militia, armed with machetes, terrorizing the village. This is the horrific reality some people face. Imagine even that you are living in a city like Beirut, a city that at least does have some prosperity, when an untended supply of ammonium nitrate explodes, killing hundreds, and leaving 300,000 homeless. And then stack the virus on top of that situation, where the hospitals are already hanging on by a thread, and now you have thousands of severely wounded victims flooding into your emergency room.

I say all of that to say this: I am incredibly grateful to be living in Canada during this incredibly trying year. Despite all of the challenges, frustrations and heartbreak we have faced, we have a lot to be grateful for.

I try as often as possible to shift my focus towards what I am grateful for in my life, as opposed to what isn't yet in my life. Here are some of my thoughts of what I'm grateful for.

Things I'm grateful for:

- Being alive
- Being healthy and free of disease; able to walk, talk, hear music, taste chocolate, hold my son in my arms and kiss my wife. Able to think and contemplate ideas, and to learn new skills
- Being free of COVID-19 (so far!) as well as all of my family being healthy and safe.
- I am grateful for the incredible front-line heroes that selflessly served people through this time, often at extreme risk to personal health and safety
- I am grateful for the scientists who worked tirelessly to produce not one but multiple vaccines to fight back against this virus
- I am grateful for living in Canada during this pandemic. There are a few other countries that have arguably handled the pandemic a little more successfully in some ways than us; but there are some that have handled the pandemic so disastrously that their government's response could be considered negligent homicide on a mass scale.
- I am grateful and proud of the Canadian government's near instantaneous financial support for those small business owners and employees hit financially during the pandemic
- I am grateful for my wife, who is the most courageous human being I know, who is so brilliant and knowing exactly the right words to say in any situation, and constantly encourages me to pursue my dreams. She was born to be a mom to our beautiful boy. She was destined for this new career, despite being adored by

every employee she leads and clients she brilliantly serves in her work
- I am grateful for my son who is the greatest source of joy in my life, for whom I have discovered unconditional love, whom I would lay my life down for; I would trade anything in my life to keep him safe and healthy
- I am grateful for my incredible family and friends who are a constant blessing and source of fun and support in my life
- I am grateful to live in a free nation; I can vote for who I want, I am free to go where I want, to practice whatever religion, marry who I want, work at what I want, and despite paying a fair bit of tax I can earn whatever I want
- I am grateful to my great friend Bill Tibbo who opened the door to my professional speaking career years ago. He has changed my life forever. I love my career, the opportunities given to me with what I do. I feel more alive on stage than anywhere else!
- I am grateful to my parents who helped shape me into the person I am today
- I am grateful to my dear mentor for many years, Dr. Steve Stokl, who guided me in learning everything I know today about success thinking, leading people and building business teams
- I am grateful for my mentor Tim Marks, who guided me in my marriage, faith and business
- I am grateful to my high-school teachers Ian Hoare, Scott Cowle, Tom Gough, and Richard Bramwell who each left an indelible mark for good in my life

- I am grateful for technology that allows me to stay in touch with everyone from loved ones to clients through this pandemic

Now that I've shared some of the things I'm grateful for, take a moment and consider how this same question applies to you: what are all the things in your life that you are grateful for, or could be? Take a few moments and write them down.

WHAT ARE YOU GRATEFUL FOR?

_____

_____

_____

_____

_____

_____

_____

_____

_____

If you want to transform your life, start every day and say, out loud, everything that you are grateful for. It immediately changes your perspective, puts you in a great mood, and arms you for any challenge the day might offer!

Despite the stress of all of the changes and added pressures, it's also important to consider: has anything good come of this year? For our family – absolutely. I've been so grateful to have so much time at home with my wife and son. Normally, I am "planes, trains and automobiles" with my work schedule, dashing all over Ontario and jumping on a plane about half a dozen times a year to zip across North America. Now, I'm doing all my presentations from home over Zoom. Not only am I enjoying the family time, I am loving my new commute. No driving anywhere! I can't believe how little gasoline I've purchased this year. I no longer get three *miles* to the gallon – I get three *months* to the gallon. Additionally, doing presentations from home, I'm not as concerned with looking all fancy, as I would on a keynote stage. Call it the "I don't care: I'm working through a pandemic" attitude. My usual attire isn't even business casual; a t-shirt and jeans is often my uniform of choice.

I remember at the beginning of the pandemic, seeing images of the cities around the world as traffic vanished, and watching in marvel as deer and other animals would start to walk down the major city streets. Smog cleared up over major metropolitan areas. It seemed like the earth, along with us all, was taking a big deep breath and pausing to find a moment of peace in the midst of all of this.

It started to feel like a year to pause, to take notice of the little things, and to feel some gratitude for what we each had. How could we not? For all the stories of people losing their businesses and incomes, and sometimes their loved ones, I was grateful to still be able to work, and work safely from home.

We would hear the stories and see the images of doctors and nurses in hospitals around the nation working on the front lines. New York, being the epicenter of virus transmission, was the perfect storm of being both an international travel hub and a densely populated city. The virus ravaged their city, and their hospital morgues were so overrun they had to stock the bodies in mobile freezer trucks in the streets. We would see the doctors and nurses break down in tears online, sharing how overwhelming this was, how hopeless they felt, how relentless and unforgiving the spread of the virus was. Some countries started making decisions about who would get ventilators, and who would be written off – there just weren't enough machines to go around. We waited with baited breath for word from the scientists who were working round the clock to create and test a vaccine.

We started seeing the best in people come out. Manufacturers sprang into action, creating personal protection equipment as fast as humanly possible. They were racing to create ventilators, to secure materials, to arrange distribution. We started cheering the front line workers in the streets: honking and cheering as each new shift of hospital workers arrived on the job. They were the heroes in the fight. I loved how we began to celebrate all of the essential workers, including truckers and delivery drivers and farmers and store clerks. Coffee shops started giving away free coffee to those on the front lines. Tim Hortons even made a coffee cup that singled out specific people who were working on the front lines; the sister of one of my friends was listed in her role as a nurse.

And we were reminded, as anyone was in a challenging time, that what is important is never the "stuff" you have, but the people you love, who love you back; the health and safety of you and your loved ones. In the crazy rush of our modern lives, we were forced to stop, to reflect, and to give thanks.

Chapter 3: Overcoming Burnout to Create Balance

"It's not the load that breaks you down, it's the way you carry it." - Lou Holtz

In April of 2002, I was given an incredible gift. It was 4:00 am, on a Saturday, I was at the office, and I was working. All four of these things in combination spelled utter disaster. And the worse part of it was that this behaviour had become the norm for me, rather than the exception. I walked into the office bathroom to splash some cold water on my face, trying anything I could to keep going, and I noticed something disturbing: a huge red mark had appeared across the top left-hand side of my forehead. It was about three inches long and an inch thick. It wasn't there yesterday, and now here it was covering half of my face. At first I was shocked, then disgusted… and then I started to get really worried. I didn't know what was happening to me. I had finally burned out.

You see, at that point, it was pretty standard for me to be working over 100 hours a week. I was waking up at 6:00 am most days, and getting home at midnight every day of the week. Some days I wouldn't even sleep at all, waking up Monday morning and going to bed Tuesday night. I didn't take vacation days; in fact, I had *never* gone on a real vacation as an adult – *not once*. Statutory holidays used to bug me because the only work I could do was paperwork (which I still don't like to this day!). Looking over my receipts, I realized that I had spent over $4500 *that year* on Wendy's hamburgers alone. I was living on fast-food and coffee, I wasn't exercising, and to top it off I had eroded many of my most important relationships. Clearly something had to give, and unfortunately what was suffering most obviously was my health.

From 1999-2002, I watched my business go up, and then I watched it start to decline with my declining health, energy and fading humour. I had starved my relationships of time and they simply faded away. I wasn't having fun anymore, which was strange since I absolutely love delivering motivational talks in front of large audiences. The greatest heartbreak of it all was when I realized in the middle of all of this that I had stopped pursuing any of my personal dreams; I was simply on a treadmill, working away towards the next business goal.

And thus, in April of 2002 I finally hit the brick wall. I had drifted away from my true passion, my health had taken a turn for the worse and I woke up from a daze to realize my life was on the wrong path.

Since I didn't have a family doctor at the time, I grudgingly went to a walk-in clinic to have the doctor on call take a look at me. I had no idea what this big burn mark on my face was: I didn't know if it was cancer, psoriasis, shingles, or hives. The doctor felt that it was probably a "stress rash". I had never heard of this, so he explained that my body wasn't designed to be living in a state of constant stress. The stress response was good for a short burst of energy to get away from a dangerous situation quickly. He used the analogy of needing to pass someone on the highway and dropping the gears on your car from 5th gear to 4th gear in order to accelerate. It's great to do for a few moments of acceleration, but you can't drive on the highway in 4th gear for too long or you'll blow the engine; the engine simply wasn't designed for that amount of stress. Neither was the human body. He said I needed to reduce my stress, get some balance, eat right and exercise, and start having some more fun in my life. If I didn't get some balance immediately, I would be headed for disaster.

I knew I had to make a change. What I was doing wasn't working. I knew I had to transform my mind, my body, my focus, the way I managed my time, the way I recharged myself. And so, I did what I'm going to encourage you to do: I made a decision to change. We only get one shot at this adventure of life, and I know you're like me: you want to make the most of it.

And so, I've chronicled the strategies that I used to turn myself around in this book. No matter who you are, these principles can be applied to make measurable, lasting change in your life experience.

What is Balance?

"Life is all about balance. You don't always need to be getting stuff done. Sometimes it's perfectly okay, and absolutely necessary, to shut down, kick back, and do nothing." – Lori Deschene

When I ask audiences this question, I'll invariably get responses that come down to dividing the amount of time between different areas of our lives; the two largest components are usually home and work. This is a good starting point, although it isn't practical. If you follow this strategy literally and balance time between each of your priorities, you'll have to divide your 24 hours between each priority evenly. If you've got 8 areas of interest, each one of them gets 3 hours. You already know that your work schedule isn't going to go down to 3 hours this week.

A nurse offered me this definition that I've found to be effective: she said that her goal was not an equitable division of *time* between each priority, but rather creating equity in *satisfaction* between each priority. Maybe you only need ten focused minutes to feel satisfied in an area, and that would get you feeling positive. If she could get a 9 out of 10 in satisfaction in each area, that would be amazing! 9 out of 10 in satisfaction in health, relationships, finance, career, and her spiritual life was her goal. I thought that this was a much more realistically achievable goal, and it's the definition I use today.

Each area of your life will require something different from you. Maybe what your life needs right now is sitting down with your kids for thirty minutes, looking them right in the eye and listening to them share everything that's going on in their world. Maybe you feel the clutter of your home office is a mental distraction, and taking ten minutes to do a quick tidy-up would bring you some positive energy. Maybe you've been feeling disconnected from a dear friend and you simply pick up the phone to say "hi." Maybe you need three hours with your spouse to have a date night and decompress. The key here is being in tune with what you feel might be missing and deciding to put a check mark next to that activity. If we start ignoring those intuitive feelings, we run the risk of wearing ourselves down.

The Crystal Balls

As I embarked on my personal journey to better understand balance and overcome burnout in my early career, I came across a powerful story by a man named Brian Dyson. He was then the CEO of Coca-Cola, and had been invited to give a commencement speech to university students. He shared:

"Imagine life as a game in which you are juggling some five balls in the air. You name them – Work, Family,

Health, Friends and Spirit and you're keeping all of these in the air.

You will soon understand that work is a rubber ball. If you drop it, it will bounce back. But the other four balls – Family, Health, Friends and Spirit – are made of glass. If you drop one of these; they will be irrevocably scuffed, marked, nicked, damaged or even shattered. They will never be the same. You must understand that and strive for it.

Work efficiently during office hours and leave on time. Give the required time to your family, friends and have proper rest. Value has a value only if its value is valued." [xlvii]

This was a transformational insight for me.

Have you ever felt this way? Have you ever felt like you were juggling multiple balls in the air, trying desperately to keep them up? I know I have. In my early career, I had mistakenly thought that career success would bring me success in every other area. All my focused effort was causing me to drop my crystal spheres on the ground.

If you drop your health sphere, everything else gets cancelled. It doesn't matter if it's a good reason or a bad one. I remember once I had a terrible pain in my gut. My sales colleague pointed and said, "I think that's your appendix. You should go to the hospital and get that checked out."

Grimacing in pain, I waved him off. "It's fine," I said through clenched teeth. "It's probably just indigestion."

He persisted. "Right there, where you are holding your gut," he said, "that's where your appendix is. And if it ruptures, let me be clear: people have died from that."

Well, that got my attention. I grudgingly headed down to the hospital, and within minutes was admitted and scheduled for emergency surgery to remove – you guessed it – my appendix. As I was being wheeled in to surgery, I was calling all of my clients and cancelling my appointments for the rest of the week. All of a sudden, the health emergency took priority over everything else.

You can also head to the hospital for a good reason. My wife was scheduled to give birth on November 14th. I remember being a young, very foolish husband, and making a big speech about how I was going to really prioritize time for her and the baby. Being self-employed, as a speaker I earn my income when I speak. I haven't had a salary in almost twenty years. The benefit of being self-employed is you can schedule off any day you want. The downside? You don't make any money that day. And, with a baby on the way and me responsible to pay the bills, I was sensitive to not cancelling too much business.

So, in my foolishness, I said to my wife, "Honey, I am going to be there for you and the baby. Big time." I took out my calendar and said, "Just let me know what day the baby is expected, and I will book the entire day off."

I am grateful my wife did not divorce me for being such a blockhead.

Her eyes narrowed as she explained that isn't how any of this works. I persisted and asked again. Exasperated, she said, "November 14th. There you go. Happy? November 14th." I smiled, thanked her, and drew a line through November 14th, blocking off the entire day. I felt very proud. (You can see where this is going, right?)

On October 23rd, as I was about to step on stage to deliver a keynote, my wife calls and says, "My water has broken. Get here now." Babies, I would come to learn, operate on their own schedule.

What about your "mental health" sphere? You realize if you drop that, everything else loses relevance quickly. We've seen so many lives lost to suicide over these last four years. My mind goes immediately to Robin Williams. Beloved by millions, adored by his family, he had incredible career success and financial abundance. He had a hit show, blockbuster movies, and had won an Oscar for Best Supporting Actor in a dramatic roll. He had everything – except his mental health. And when you lose that, it doesn't matter if you have a mansion and Lamborghinis, family and fame, cash in the bank and exotic vacations. You don't care. And so we need to treat our mental health as a cherished crystal sphere that we need to nurture and protect, and seek out professional support when needed.

What about our relationships? If you are going through a major relationship issue, you know how futile it is to try and compartmentalize that. You carry the storm cloud above you through your workday, and into your night. With isolation through the pandemic, if you are married or living together, you can't even get respite from the tension by going to a physical office. Relationship problems drain us in so many ways. We can't just work all day and ignore them – we have to cherish and nurture those special relationships. That includes spouses, kids, extended family, and friends.

The trick to all of this is recognizing that each area of our life is significant and requires attention. We can't devote our resources to one area, starve the other, and expect things to work out. We need to make steps – even baby steps if that's all we have to give in the moment – to repair those damaged areas.

"Escape" is not Balance

"Life is like riding a bicycle. To keep your balance, you must keep moving." – Albert Einstein

Many people mistakenly believe that balance means "getting away" from life: getting away from the stress of work, from family obligations, and getting some serious R'n'R down-time.

You can spot these people because their bumper sticker reads "TGIF": Thank Goodness It's Friday. Pre-COVID, these people would be lacing up their running shoes, assuming a crouched position around 4:58pm every Friday afternoon and hoping to hear the starter pistol fire at 5:00, so that they could bolt to freedom! They would celebrate all Friday and Saturday... but by Sunday night their tummy started to tighten into a knot, because they knew that they had to go back and face the expected stress of Monday morning.

The next strategy for the escapist is to continue to believe that "escape" works, but you need more time than just a two-day weekend. This person says, "I'm so stressed... I need to go on a vacation!" You can spot these people because they have screensavers on their computer with pictures of palm trees, beaches and dolphins. They also have a calendar beside their computer with big black X's crossed through each day that passes; they are counting down the days till they get to escape! Finally, the big day comes. And what's interesting is that people are in such a great mood the day before a vacation, that their energy and spirits are up and they are highly motivated to get so much work done so it is off their plate for a week!

This person goes on vacation, and it takes them a couple of days to unwind. By Tuesday they actually succeed in leaving their iPhone in their hotel room. By Thursday, they are down by the poolside, sipping margaritas and doing the limbo. But by Saturday, they start to get that sickening feeling in their stomach because they know that they have to return to the thing that is stressing them out back at home. Over and over, we see that the escape strategy *just doesn't work*.

Let me acknowledge that it is valuable to have a fun weekend, and it's great to go on a vacation. A "strategic sabbatical" certainly has its place in your journey. But an escapist vacation doesn't change anything in your life that is stressing you out. A vacation is like an Aspirin; it merely masks the pain without addressing the underlying cause of the headache. If you have a headache because you haven't eaten, or because you are suffering sinus congestion, an Aspirin neither fills your belly nor blows your nose for you. It just buys you a few hours of being able to ignore the problem. But problems don't go away when you ignore them; in fact, they usually get worse.

What you need to do is address the problem. Confront it, head on, and fix it. You need to name it, figure out what caused it, create a solution, and execute your strategy. Hoping that the problem will just go away if you ignore it is called the "Ostrich Manoeuvre"; you just bury your head in the sand so you can't see what's happening. From this moment on, I want to encourage you to confront your problems with vigor and excise them from your life. We could choose *any day* to lift our energy and spirits to accomplish the same result; we don't need a vacation to do it.

Today Is Your Whole Life

"This is the beginning of a new day. You have been given this day to use as you will. You can waste it or use it for good. What you do today is important because you are exchanging a day of your life for it. When tomorrow comes, this day will be gone forever; in its place is something that you have left behind. Let it be something good." – Mac Anderson

I've come to realize that our lives are simply a collection of single days. In order to create a masterpiece of your life, you must discover your personal recipe for having one exceptional day. Then, repeat the process seven times in a row and you've created an amazing week. Do it fifty-two-times in a row and you've got an incredible year, and do it over and over and you're going to be living an exceptional life. The building block for an exceptional *life* is an exceptional *day*.

The reason that you want to focus on making today an exceptional experience is because tomorrow never comes. Many people procrastinate on improving their lives and say to themselves, "I will exercise… just not today! I'll do it tomorrow." Except that tomorrow never comes: when you wake up "tomorrow", it will have been renamed "today". Everything we do will happen during a today; every action we take to further our cause and achieve our goals will happen during a "today". Your marriage will improve during a today, your finances will improve during a today, your mood and emotions will change during a today. Today is your whole life.

What does a "great day" during the pandemic look like for you? Take a moment where you describe this ideal day. It might include things you want to add, like relaxing activities, or things you want to remove, like stressors and energy drains. Describe what ingredients are in your great day:

_____
_____
_____
_____
_____
_____
_____
_____

Oxygen Mask

"You can't pour from an empty cup. Take care of yourself first."
– Unknown

Whenever we take an airplane for travel, the stewardesses invariably go through the safety demonstration, showing us how to properly use our seatbelts, the oxygen masks, the inflatable life preservers under our seat, and where the emergency exits are located. Every plane I've been on, I've endured the video demonstration of these procedures. They invariably mention what to do when a parent and a small child are sitting together. The oxygen masks were shown to descend, and everyone was supposed to put them on. My question to you is:

Who is supposed to put the mask on first: the parent, or the child?

To anyone who has flown, we know the answer: the parent is supposed to put the mask on first. Why is that, do you suppose? Because the child cannot help the parent; the parent must take care of the child. In fact, we are warned that if we are traveling with anyone who is elderly or handicapped, the same rule applies: we put the mask on ourselves first. We recognize intellectually that this is the correct action, but that doesn't make it any easier if it is your child! In fact, the natural instinct of every parent is to take care of their child first, and take care of themselves LAST. But if we do that in this situation, what happens? We risk becoming overwhelmed by the smoke, losing consciousness, and since our child depends on us to get them to safety, we're both in trouble.

The moral of the lesson is this: in order to be able to take care of everyone else, you must take care of yourself FIRST.

Rank Your Priorities

Right now, I'd like you to brainstorm the top-ten priorities in your life. Put everything down that is important to you: family, work, volunteering… everything.

OVERCOMING BURNOUT TO CREATE BALANCE

Name of Priority	# of Hours	Rank

1. _____

2. _____

3. _____

4. _____

5. _____

6. _____

7. _____

8. _____

9. _____

10. _____

Now that you've listed each of the priorities, under the column labeled "Rank", please rank each priority according to the number of hours each week you spend on it. For example, work will likely be near the top of the list, as most people spend 35-60 hours a week working. Whatever gets the most number of hours, please place a #1 under the "Rank" column, followed by #2 for whatever activity gets the second most number of hours, and on down the line.

The reason I like to rank priorities according to time is because time is a finite resource, and so we will only invest it in the things that we feel are important. Many people say that they have a priority in a certain area, but their calendar says otherwise. For example, someone may say that their kids are a priority, but when they audit their own calendar they realize that they only spend a few minutes each day talking to their children.

When I do this exercise I ask the audience how many people put "work" on the list. Everyone puts up their hand. Then I ask how many people put some variation on the theme of "relationships" on the list, either spouse, kids, extended family or friends. Again, nearly everyone puts up their hand. Then I ask a third and potentially devastating question:

"How many people put themselves on the list?" Fully half to two-thirds of my audiences do not put themselves on the list of priorities in their own lives. It's no wonder that so many people feel totally out of balance! They aren't even a priority to themselves. Most people take care of everyone but themselves, and then they come to my seminar and wonder why they feel out of balance!

The Young Lumberjack

There's a fable of a young lumberjack getting started on a new job site. Full of vim and vigor, this young guy is determined to make an amazing impression on his new boss. He asks around, "Who is the very best lumberjack on the job site?" He is pointed towards Dave, an experienced lumberjack. The young lumberjack asks the veteran,

"How many trees can you chop down each day?"

Dave looks at him thoughtfully and replies, "Ten. I chop down ten trees, every single day."

Now that the young lumberjack has a clear goal in mind, he sets off to impress everyone. Working vigorously through the day, he manages to cut down fifteen trees! He is very proud of himself and he shares his accomplishment with Dave, who once again cut down exactly ten trees. "Well done," says Dave with a knowing smile.

The next morning, the young lumberjack heads right to the tree line to begin chopping. However, today it seems a little harder. He is making less progress, feeling like it's taking more effort to get the same work done. He is really breaking into a sweat, and is dismayed to find out that he only chopped down twelve trees. Dave, once again, only cut down ten trees.

Now he is annoyed. He resolves to make the third day count. He comes an hour early, and gets busy. While he is working his guts out, he notices Dave is sipping his coffee, reading a book! *What a slacker*, the young lumberjack thought. Collapsing in exhaustion at the end of the day, he is incredibly frustrated to discover that he has only cut down eight trees that day... even less than Dave!

That's it, he says to himself. I'm going to show that old timer who the superstar is around here. The young lumberjack arrives early, works through lunch, doesn't take a break all day, and works as the other men depart for the day. As the final rays of sunlight are fading, the young lumberjack is forced to throw in the towel, having now only cut down six trees. He staggers past the exit gate, and notices on the work board that, once again, Dave has cut down ten trees.

Overcome with frustration and exhaustion, the young lumberjack collapses in bed. This doesn't make any sense, he mutters to himself as he tries to slip into sleep. How is it possible that I am working harder than Dave, yet I keep getting worse and worse results? He decides to ask Dave the next morning.

As the men arrive on the jobsite the next day, the young lumberjack spots Dave arriving. He approaches him, now a little embarrassed by his earlier arrogance.

"Hey Dave," he says, a little sheepishly. "Can I ask you a quick question?"

"Sure thing," Dave replies, unscrewing his Thermos to enjoy a little coffee at the start of his workday.

"Well, I suppose I am a little confused. I see that each day, I am working harder and harder, and yet I am getting less and less done. On the other hand, I watch you take your time, take breaks, and still manage to consistently chop down ten trees a day. What's going on?"

Dave smiles. "It's really simple," he explains. "And, I've got great news for you: you can get the same results that I do. Here's all we are doing differently. First, I really admire your work ethic. Boy, you are putting in some great effort! Coming early, skipping lunch, staying late. But," he says, pointing to his tools, "each day while you are working harder and harder, I actually do something different. I take a break, every single day… and I *sharpen my axe.*"

The poor young lumberjack was working with a blade that grew duller every day! No wonder he was making less and less progress. In fact, he was making a mistake that now seems obvious to us as we read the story. But, how often would we admit that we make the same mistake? That we think the solution to our problems is just to push the gas pedal down further?

Sometimes, the actual solution to a problem feels counterintuitive. For example, when a plane stalls and starts falling downward, what do you suppose our natural inclination is to do?

We want to pull up. And, while that feeling is understandable, doing so would get you killed.

The actual correct solution is to push the stick down.[xlviii] Down! Forcing the plane to go faster towards the ground! This would be terrifying to experience: the ground is already rushing up at you, and all your senses tell you that you're in mortal danger. And yet, by pushing the stick down, you gain speed and lift, and are then able to safely pull out of it.

When life feels like it's spinning out of control, when we are overwhelmed by pressure and deadlines and stress and problems, we can sometimes react the same way: to push harder. To skip lunch. To skip exercise. To skip healthy foods. To skip pausing to catch our breath. And, while skipping those things because we are "busy" might seem intuitive, they actually send us crashing down even faster.

STRATEGIC BREAKS

With our lives feeling so busy, it's critical to find a way to fit balance into a schedule that already seems stuffed to the brim. You're already juggling taking care of family, homeschooling your kids, getting your work done while figuring out how to work with a remote team, keeping the house running, dropping off groceries to your 76-year-old mom, checking that your elderly relatives are getting their COVID-19 vaccines… and somehow you're supposed to find time for balance?

I realize it can feel daunting, almost impossible on some days, to carve out time for you. What I found that works for me is breaking it into manageable baby steps. Can you carve out 5 minutes? Start with that. What I have found that works for me is to divide balance breaks into three separate time categories, and make sure each one gets starts to get some attention. Those categories are:

1. Daily Rituals – Your 5-Minute Joy Break
2. Weekly Escapes – Your Purposeful Hobby
3. Annual Adventures – Getting Away From It All

We don't need to escape from our lives or put them on hold – we want to build recharging activities into the fabric of our daily experience. In time, these practices shift away from something you have to remind yourself to do, and become a welcome

Daily Rituals - The 5-Minute Recharge

One of the key strategies that I've learned (mostly through trial and error!) is the ability to take the precious moments we have and squeeze the most juice out of each one of them. So here is a powerful question to consider:

If you only had 5 minutes, what could you do to recharge?

Everyone always thinks that they need a HUGE break, sitting at the spa for days on end and being bathed in mud that has magical healing properties or lying face down and getting hot rocks placed on their back. This is the image of I see in countless print ads for spa retreats as the ultimate vision of balance. Excellent, if you have the time, money or inclination to go to a hot-rock-and-mud spa retreat – let alone if they are even accepting clients during COVID. I'm sure they are excellent balancing activities, but the problem I have with these strategies is that they demand that you pull yourself OUT of your normal, daily routine. My point is that balance needs to be part of your daily and weekly routine. You don't drive your car when the engine light turns on or indicates you are out of oil, but we think nothing of driving ourselves when we are running on empty. The big problem for people with balance would be solved if we all had a warning light that went off when we were pushing ourselves too far.

You need to figure out how to recharge your batteries in 5 minutes. You need to brainstorm a list of personal recharge activities that you can realistically add to your schedule and make it part of your daily life experience. Taking care of yourself is not a once-a-year thing when you escape to Maui; balance is as necessary as food and water.

The key is that you need to reward yourself, every day, with moments of renewal. By identifying key strategies that are quick and simple, it's more likely that you'll be able to sprinkle them liberally throughout your daily experience.

Here are some examples to get you started:

Daily 5-minute Joy Breaks

- ❑ Read
- ❑ Listen to your favorite music
- ❑ Get up and dance!
- ❑ Exercise of any kind
- ❑ Cook your favorite food
- ❑ Go for a walk

- ❑ Go for a run around the block, or a bike ride down the street and back
- ❑ Engage in random acts of kindness
- ❑ Compliment a friend or a colleague on a job well done
- ❑ Talk to friends
- ❑ Read or watch something funny
- ❑ Share a joke with a friend
- ❑ Play a musical instrument: piano, guitar, drums, singing
- ❑ Keep healthy snacks at your desk: fruit, sliced veggies, water
- ❑ Play with your kids
- ❑ Snuggle on the couch with your spouse
- ❑ Get some healthy "Brain Exercise" – play some games on brain-focus apps like *Lumosity*, *Elevate*, or *Chess.com*
- ❑ Listen to audios in your time through the day, and before and after work
  - o Motivational & Self-Improvement
  - o Business Audio Books
  - o Fiction audio books
  - o Comedy
- ❑ Manage your physiology
  - o Exercise
  - o Deep breathing
  - o Progressive muscle relaxation
  - o Meditation and visualization
  - o Stand up and stretch
  - o Yoga
  - o Pilates
- ❑ Have an unwinding Ritual at the end of the day:
  - o Hot bubble bath
  - o Read in bed

- Enjoy some relaxing music
- Cup of chamomile tea

This list is just a starting point. Think of your own ideas. What could you do to have some fun, to relax yourself, to energize yourself, to recharge yourself? When I did this activity for myself, I came up with my own list of balancing activities. I realize that the things that I find balancing might be the polar opposite of what you find balancing. For example, I don't like gardening, baking, or sitting on the porch. However, I absolutely recognize that these are very popular activities for many people. There is no right or wrong answer with balance; the only criterion is whether or not the activity makes *you* feel good.

Take a moment and write down every activity, every hobby, every person, every place that makes you feel good and brings you happiness and energy.

Sometimes people are stumped on this, because it's been so long since you've taken the time to have some fun. So another question to ask is **"What did you used to do for fun, before you got so busy?"** Did you have any old hobbies that you loved but you have dropped, or do you dream of any new hobbies that you'd like to start?

Now that you've got some activities identified, I'd like to encourage you to set the goal of doing at least one of the DAILY activities each and every day of your life. You'll immediately begin to feel better, certainly because you know that you are honouring yourself and taking time for you… and you deserve it.

Mindfullness

"The little things? The little moments? They aren't little." – Jon Kabat-Zinn

Want a fast and powerful way to cleanse yourself of stress, reclaim your mental focus and bring some energy back into your daily experience – in just a few minutes? Pause for a moment and concentrate deeply on your present moment, without judgment. That's the entire essence of mindfulness, a mental-health strategy championed by Dr. Jon Kabat-Zinn of the University of Massachusetts.[xlix] It's a wellness philosophy thousands of years old but has enjoyed a resurgence of attention and popularity in recent years. Mindfullness is not philosophically connected to any religion and has no specific spiritual undertones, though it is often attributed as religious in nature. It is a practice of quieting your mind and increasing your focus – something that we can all benefit from in our interruption-addled days.

How do you do it? You simply focus intently on the present moment, but with a detached emotional experience – just as you would if you were watching a video of someone else. Your cognitive experience, if translated into words might be, "I notice I am sitting in my chair. I notice my breathing is slow, deep and relaxed. I notice the sound of the traffic outside. I notice that my hands are unclenched. I notice the tension in my furrowed eyebrows. I notice the texture of the armrest against my fingertips. I notice I find my mind racing. I notice I am experiencing my mind quieting. I notice a feeling of peace spreading throughout my mind and body."

You are just noticing, intently, without judgment. That's a critical component of mindfulness – that absolute lack of judgment. You aren't saying "I notice tension in me – what's wrong with me that I can't handle this?" or "I notice I am low energy – what was I thinking, staying up so late?" These are judgmental thoughts. Gently lead yourself away from any analysis of what you are experiencing.

People who regularly engage in mindfulness report greater feelings of peace, lowered stress, and greater mental focus – a powerful selling point for knowledge workers facing "brain fog" through COVID-19.

Fortunately, there are some fantastic resources available through www.mindful.org, as well as apps such as *Calm* or *Headspace* that can assist with mindfulness. You can find a veritable ocean of free content available online through YouTube. Give it a try and see if you enjoy the benefits.

Create a "Recharge" Zone

"What if we recharged ourselves as often as we recharge our phones?" – Unknown

So many people dream of going to the spa to recharge… why don't you do it in your own home! If possible, designate a place in your home that is your "balance" zone. This could be a separate room, the sofa or the armchair with great books to read, your guest bedroom, or the bathtub that you line with candles and soak in a luxurious hot bubble bath while reading a great book. Try if possible to keep this area free of clutter, free of work, and free of bills or documents that distract your attention and potentially create tension. Create a miniature oasis if possible. Is there something you could do to decorate this space or increase your comfort? Perhaps including a motivational or positive picture quote, a plant, or maybe a diffuser that releases a relaxing spray into the room?

Since so many roles are overlapping during the pandemic, having your own little corner is even more important. With our "office" really being our bedroom, and our kid's "classroom" being the dining table, this is even more important. Where in your house can you claim for your personal oasis? I understand that every family situation is different, and my suggesting you have a little niche might be easier said than done. You might have eight people jammed into three rooms – I get it. I remember my wife recounting the story of escaping to the bathroom for peace and quiet, and upon exiting she found our then two-year-old and both cats waiting patiently outside the door for her to come back out. The bathroom was the one room she could lock the door and be alone! Your oasis might literally be going out to the car, driving around the corner and enjoying a coffee while you listen to music and lean the seat back.

In our home, my office doubles as my oasis (though it unfortunately it also contains my work and my bills!). It has a small flight of stairs that separates it from the rest of the upstairs. I've got a loveseat and a special massage chair that I love to sit in and read. My office also has a miniature fireplace that creates an incredible experience in the winter, and it is directly across from my couch. I keep my library of books in my office as well as my piano, and it truly is my sanctuary in my home to clear my thoughts. I have motivational statements written on the wall that energize me, as well as pictures I've collected that I use to visualize the ideal future I'm creating for myself and my family. All of things are energizing to me and help me feel centered and powerful.

Create a "Bounce" in Your Day

"Today's goals: coffee and kindness. Maybe two coffees, and then kindness." – Nanea Hoffman

I'll bet you've had days where you had a bounce in your step – you felt upbeat, cheerful, and things were going your way. What caused this? Really think back and dig through some of these memories.

I'll bet some of them were **accomplishments**: your boss or client complimented you, your proposal got accepted, you landed the sale, or you got the promotion. That's exciting!

Some of these were **connections**: you did something nice for someone else, like a random act of kindness, or someone helped you out and you were thankful and relieved. It could also be romantic: maybe your sweetheart sent you an exciting message that got your heart racing.

Some of these days were big life events: you got engaged. You saw the ultrasound of your first baby! You wheeled up to your new home and opened the door with your key for the very first time as proud homeowners.

Some of these were activity-based: you'd had a fun weekend and were reminiscing about the adventures you enjoyed. You'd started into a new online class and were excited about what you were learning. You were planning on holding a virtual party at your home that night for friends and you were all going to cook together.

Maybe it's something as simple as "retail therapy." You treated yourself to a little present – a nice pastry at the shop, a new book from Amazon, or a cool electronic gadget you've had your eye on for months. (Or in my wife's case – new shoes!)

Maybe you had finally said "yes" to something that has your tummy all tied up in excited butterflies. You've said "yes" to leading a class, or giving a speech, or tackling a new project at work that will be a stretch-goal and get you noticed.

Whatever that neat recipe was for you – be intentional with recreating it! Could you on-purpose say, "Wow, I feel great right now. I need to make sure I do this again."

I'll tell you one thing that is a bit of a "bounce" activity for our teenage son is getting to stay up late and have fun (which for him, is video games with friends and watching a movie.) For him, it's part of his experience when he's on Christmas break or a vacation. Is it a perfect strategy for long term health and wellness? Nope. Does it make our kid happier right now? You bet. In fact, just this week, we let him take the entire day off school to play his favorite game Fortnite. There was a big announcement of a new season, and he was excited to watch the live event. We made him a deal: as long as all his homework was done by that day and he was caught up on all his assignments, he could take the day off. He got it done, got the day off, and was super happy. Does missing a day of school ruin his career chances? Nope. There is no hiring manager that will ask him about his Grade 8 experience. But if we can find some non-damaging little experience to bring some sunlight into his day during this pandemic, we're definitely considering it. I am sure there are many parenting books out there that might disagree with this strategy. My thought is if something is working for you and your family, keep doing it. It doesn't matter if some article I read in the paper describes another SuperMom or

WonderDad who is amazing at doing Martha Stewart crafts with her kids, having them tucked neatly into bed on time, etc. Bedtime for us these days is whenever we feel ready. If Braydon wants to stay up and have fun, we're letting him have more flexibility. I might go back to being Mr. Tough Dad after the pandemic, but these days, we're simply being a little more relaxed about stuff. I think part of this is to get through each day guilt-free that you are doing your best, and that's okay.

What's something you could do in the next 24-hours to put some bounce in your day? Identify that, and if it makes sense, try to do more of that action each day.

High Performers Need a Break

"There are 1,440 minutes in one day, so taking 5 of those minutes to re-energize will not be the end of the world." – Unknown

Some people reading this are naturally going to resist the idea of taking a break, because they are a self-proclaimed workaholic superstar. I get it – I've been there. It's no surprise that I really struggled with this concept back in my original sales career. I actually believed that taking a break meant that I was lazy, that I wasn't committed, that my business would go backwards if I took the foot off the pedal, and I was committed to always pushing myself to the limits. But everyone around me, most especially the top sales performers, warned me constantly that I needed to take at least a day every week and do nothing but relax. That included housework, because housework is still work.

There is a fallacious belief in many corporate cultures that people who take a lunch break neither want, nor deserve, a promotion. You can see this belief is put into action when everyone who wants a promotion starts working through lunch. Let me be clear: with rare exception, working through lunch is generally a terrible strategy – and it's an absolutely devastating long-term strategy. Here's why.

Answer me this: if you are exhausted, does it take you *longer* to complete a task? You bet it does. How about this: do you tend to make more *errors* when you are exhausted? Yes again.

Now, if I ask you whether or not you feel refreshed after a break, the answer is almost always yes (unless you felt guilty during the break about the fact that you were having a break, and you ruined it for yourself… or the activity you engaged in wasn't that renewing for you.)

What is amazing is that if you skip lunch, you're both physically depleted (because you didn't eat or rest for even a minute) and mentally drained (because you didn't clear your mind). It ends up taking you 8 hours to do 6 hours of work, because you start slowing down as the day wears on. However, if you had just taken a break, you could have been refreshed. Wouldn't it make sense to take a short break, recharge your batteries, and then attack your afternoon fully refreshed? You'll get more done in a shorter period of time.

All of this is can be described as The Law of Diminishing Returns. The point of this law is that after a certain point of effort, you get less and less output for the time and energy you invest. For example, if you work 40 hours, you'll get 40 hours of productivity. If you work 50 hours, maybe you'll be productive for 35 hours. If you work 60 hours, maybe you'll be productive for 30 hours. And down it goes.

Years ago, I consulted with a marketing agency, and they had made a really interesting discovery about the performance of their employees. Because of their technology, they were able to very accurately track how much work was getting done and when. Not surprisingly, they found that through the summertime, Friday afternoons were a wasteland of employee unproductivity. So, they rolled out a really ingenious idea: they told people that if they got their work done early, they could leave early, between 1-3pm Friday afternoon. Suddenly, employees who were languishing were now outperforming their previous best efforts in order to earn some time off – and morale soared as a by-product. The point? Stop thinking of a high-performing employee as someone who works till 10pm Friday. Instead, consider it the sign of a high-performing employee that they happily get their work done by 1pm Friday so they can earn the afternoon off to rest and play – and come back to work Monday even more refreshed and rarin' to go.

A final thought – this strategy is a great strategy to race out of the proverbial door at 1pm on a Friday for the reward of getting home. But through COVID-19, we are *already* at home. There is no hard deadline where we need to leave the office. Because of this, work can easily bleed into your evening and weekend time. You can say, "I've done enough for a Friday – I'll just catch up on this work on Saturday afternoon." There just isn't the same hard stop that is forced by your environment. So, you need to create a self-imposed "hard stop." Taking a break not only includes little 5-minute recharges, and a lunch break – it also means that work needs to come to a dead stop on the by the weekend. That might mean you push yourself a little harder on Friday so that you can keep your weekend clear for family time and personal renewal. Exactly – that's how we did it before the pandemic.

Weekly Escapes – Your Purposeful Hobby

"I never know what to say when people ask me what my hobbies are. I mean, I'm a MOM. I enjoy trips to the bathroom alone and in silence." – Anonymous

I firmly believe that absolutely everyone needs a break each week with zero responsibilities, where you can do whatever fun, relaxing or rewarding task you wish. It seems though that men seem to have an easier time claiming this for themselves than Mom's. Men seem more often to stand up for themselves, perhaps out of selfishness, or perhaps because they don't carry around the same unfortunate guilt that Mom's do. But Mom's need a break!

Every single week, you should schedule time in your calendar that is YOUR TIME OFF. That means: you don't help anyone else do anything. You don't cook, clean, help with homework… nothing. You simply relax and have fun! This is where your "Weekly Escape" activities can be scheduled. I'm especially talking to Mom's here: this is your time to putter in the garden, to window shop, to hang out with your friends, to rock climb, play the drums, paint, or anything else you want to do! You must schedule this and protect it as a sacred meeting and only the most dire of emergencies should override your time for yourself.

What could you do for fun with 5 uninterrupted hours? Would you paint? Sing? Decorate? Exercise? It really is up to you.

Perhaps you are thinking, "CJ, I am a single mom. There is no one else to take care of the kids – to handle responsibilities around the house – how am I supposed to do this? This just isn't realistic for my personal situation."

My heart sincerely goes out to you. I do realize that everyone faces different challenges. My mom was a single mom as I grew up, as was my mother-in-law. I appreciate the reality of the challenge. If (God forbid) my wife passed away, here's what I would do in this situation. I would arrange time on a weekly basis for someone to come to my home, watch my son, while I had scheduled time for me to recharge. That could be grandparents coming over to babysit. That could be dropping my son off at his cousins house for a fun afternoon. That could be enrolling him in a public class run at the community centre for a few hours. It could be a babysitter if that makes sense for the budget. If none of those options were available, I would arrange with another parent to have their child over for a play-date this weekend with son, and next weekend, my son goes and plays at their house for the afternoon.

Remember also that for people working from home through COVID-19, the time they would have spent commuting is now "found time" in their schedule. How long was your old commute to and from work? This is time that you can reclaim for yourself.

What could be some of those hobbies you would enjoy if you had a couple of hours on your own? Some of these activities are pre- and post-COVID (as we will all still need balance when the pandemic is over) and some will be modified versions of those fun activities, as we find a way to do them from the safety of our home. What hobbies and weekly escapes will you enjoy?

- ❑ Gardening
- ❑ Learn a new language – try apps like Duolingo

- ❑ Online classes for the fun of the subject
- ❑ If you're feeling trapped at home, you can still pick a recipe, enjoy the experience of making the meal together, and have a candlelit dinner at the dining table.
- ❑ Have an online movie watch party with friends
- ❑ Have an online dinner party with friends, where you all cook the same recipe simultaneously and dig in together
- ❑ Creative work:
    - o Paint & drawing
    - o Singing
    - o Compose music
    - o Creative writing
    - o Computer animation
    - o Home renovation
    - o Woodworking
    - o Arts and crafts
- ❑ Volunteer Work
    - o Habitat For Humanity
    - o Big Brothers/ Big Sisters
    - o Local Hospital
    - o Women's Shelter
    - o Animal Hospital
    - o Challenge Day
    - o …or any cause you are passionate about!
- ❑ Sports (post-COVID):
    - o Joining a running club
    - o Ultimate Frisbee
    - o Softball League
    - o Hockey
    - o Flag Football
    - o Soccer
    - o Dragon Boat racing

What is your favorite hobby that you'd like to spend more time doing, or even a new hobby that you'd like to pick up? Maybe there is a hobby that you used to do before you got so busy, that it's time to pick up again and circle back to your passion. What is it?

Have an Annual Adventure

I created the concept of an annual adventure for myself because I was finding that each year started to seem the same as the last. It was all a grey wash of meetings, driving fast all over the city, collapsing in bed, and starting over… with no sign of a break in sight.

You want to have something big and exciting scheduled this year that you are looking forward to. You want to create a memory that stands out in your mind and defines the magic of that year. When you look back on each year, you want these adventures to be some of the greatest memories you've created.

What would you do with a week off? Would you travel? Go camping? The choices are limitless! Some people say that they don't have the money to go on the vacation they want. I always say to everyone that they should set aside a few dollars from each paycheque into a vacation fund. Even $50 off of each paycheque would equal $6000 in 5 years. What sort of vacation would that pay for? It would certainly be amazing and create some remarkable memories! Take action now on planning these exciting adventures for yourself to make this one of the most memorable years of your life!

Since travel has been affected by COVID, it's natural to think "I'm not even going to allow myself to think about these things until everything has settled down." I understand – and I still think it's a good idea to imagine future possibilities that are fun and exciting, so you have something wonderful to look forward to through the year!

Vacations
- ☐ Go camping
- ☐ Weekend bed-and-breakfast
- ☐ Wine tasting tour though vineyards
- ☐ Rent an RV and see go cross-country
- ☐ Disney World with the kids
- ☐ Caribbean resort vacation
- ☐ Travel Europe by train
- ☐ Enjoy your dream vacation to Australia
- ☐ Go on a cruise to the Mediterranean
- ☐ … or to Alaska!

Charity
- ☐ Missionary work
- ☐ Teach at a school in Kenya
- ☐ Run a charity marathon

Adventures

- ☐ Mountain climbing
- ☐ BMW race school
- ☐ Skydiving

- ☐ Bungee Jumping
- ☐ White-water rafting
- ☐ Play the best golf courses in the world
- ☐ Rappel down the side of an office tower
- ☐ Do the EDGE Walk around the CN Tower
- ☐ Indoor skydiving

WHAT'S MISSING? TACKLING YOUR ENERGY DRAINS

Sometimes, the easiest way to begin to change things is to decide what you DON'T want. Maybe it's been years since you've articulated what you secretly desire in your career, finances, relationships or fitness level… but when asked, you can immediately define what you are tired of experiencing.

And so, beside each priority, I'd like you to take a moment and answer just that. What isn't working as well as it could? What is the "problem", if you wish to use that word? What frustrates or disappoints you? What do you feel is lacking? What are you sick and tired of?

Of course, this need not be pessimistic. If things are already going well, what could be improved in each area? Maybe you've got a good marriage, but you want to make it great. Maybe you've got great finances, but you want to make them exceptional. I'm a firm believer that we can always improve anything… in fact, we should endeavour to do the best we can in every area of our life!

So, what is missing in your life?

- ➢ Maybe you and your spouse love each other, but it feels like you are two ships passing in the night. You spend so much time and energy at work, then you race home to take care of the kids and clean the house… by the time you have any time alone, you've got no energy left to enjoy each other!

- ➢ Maybe you have a good job, but you've grown restless. It's been quite a while since you've felt challenged. You have a hunger to learn and grow; you want to see a clear path to promotion, and you crave the opportunity to show your company the talents that lay dormant inside you

- ➢ Maybe what's missing is time for yourself. You feel like you spend all of your energy taking care of the people around you, and you have nothing left. Maybe you used to have a favorite hobby before the kids were born, but it's been years since you've taken the time to enjoy that hobby. Maybe you used to be involved in a sports team before you got that promotion at work, but with so many late nights at the office it's been months since you've had a little fun.

- ➢ Maybe what's missing is financial abundance… or even financial security. Maybe you've dreamed of an incredible vacation, but you never seem to have the cash. Maybe you arrive at the end of your money before you arrive at the end of the month. Maybe making the mortgage payment is always a struggle, and the fridge seems a little too bare. Every time something breaks, it feels like an emergency. You worry that the car will need repairs, or the roof will need to be fixed. You are sick of saying "no" to your kids every time they want to start a hobby or go on a school trip. Maybe you look at your credit card statement, or your mortgage amortization chart, and you have a sick feeling that at this rate, it's going to be a long time before you dig yourself out of debt.

➢ Maybe you work a midnight shift at your job and you arrive home just as your family is leaving for the day. You are physically exhausted from having to change your body clock each week… and it seems like you never have the quality time with your friends and family that you want

➢ Maybe you've had a check-up with the doctor, and the news wasn't good. The test came back positive. Maybe your blood pressure is too high, or your cholesterol level is too high. Maybe your children are learning to ride a bicycle, but you struggle to even run beside them without gasping for air. Maybe it's a struggle to even find the energy to climb up a flight of stairs. Your pant size keeps expanding with your waist. You look at photos of yourself from a few years ago and wonder where that younger, healthier, more vibrant person went.

➢ Maybe you feel disconnected from your kids. The time you spend with them feels transactional, and as they are getting older you mourn the closeness you enjoyed when they were younger. You wish that they would trust you to talk with you about anything and everything in their lives; you know that you've got so much wisdom, experience and love to share with them. But so many conversations these days are reduced to one-word answers, dinner conversation is stale, and they just want to borrow the car keys to hang out with their friends. You miss them.

➢ Maybe your parents are aging, and you have brought one or both of them to live with you because the alternative of a long-term care facility is just not an option for them. You love your parents, but you hadn't planned on being a caregiver at this stage in your life. You thought that once your kids were grown up and out of the house, your schedule would open up… but you've now got a second full-time job, and you're burning out.

➢ Maybe you feel worried all of the time. You just have a gnawing sense of foreboding that things are slipping away, that everything that can go wrong will go wrong, and that bad times are coming. You don't even remember what it feels like to just relax, smile and feel content; it feels like everything could fall apart at any moment.

➢ Maybe you have woken up and realized that your life isn't what you wanted it to be. You know that you are capable of doing more, of being more, of having more… and yet something is holding you back. Maybe fear, maybe doubt, maybe sadness… but the dreams you had as a kid haven't materialized, and you wish life were more exciting.

These examples are just a small sample of the common struggles that many people face, every day of their lives. Admittedly, I've left off the list any examples of major tragedies, such as the loss of a spouse or child, financial ruin, or a debilitating illness. Anyone in one of these situations has the challenge they face at the forefront of their mind and does not need to brainstorm in order to articulate it. But the great majority of people need to be reminded of what isn't working, and why.

I've got great news for you: every single life situation that is challenging has a remedy; it's just that the answer may not be obvious to us at first glance. In fact, the answer might be obvious, but we might choose to avoid making the necessary change because it is too uncomfortable in the short-term.

What problems are you facing in each area? What are you no longer willing to tolerate in your life? What is happening in your life, regardless of the pandemic, that you are fed up with?

Relationships (spouse, kids, friends, family)

Finances

Career

Health (diet/exercise)
___

Mental/Emotional Health
___

Volunteer Work
___

Hobbies/Leisure
___

It's understandable that the pandemic is probably going to add additional pressure in each area of your life that is already facing challenges. Great – now let's start to fix it. While I do love setting aspirational goals where you reach for something magnificent and inspiring, I also believe that there is a place for setting goals to fix problems – the yucky, unpleasant or even awful things that we suffer through in our lives. And even in those circumstances, there is something you can control.

Relationships

Whether it's your spouse, intimate partner, parents, friend, siblings, neighbors, coworkers or boss, relationship issues are a major energy drain. All the happy movies, yoga and deep breathing in the world isn't going to fix a major relationship problem either at home or work.

On occasion I am asked to sit down with couples (though I am not a marriage counselor by training) and help them get things on the right path. When I ask them what's going on, do you suppose each person lays the blame at their own feet, pointing out the mistakes they personally made and how they personally need to improve? Not really. Most of the finger pointing and blame is aimed right at the other person, and all the justification and defensiveness rests with the person talking.

A friend loaned me a movie called *Fireproof*, starring Kirk Cameron. It's a Christian movie, so it won't be to everyone's taste or beliefs, but it had a really great message and a simple strategy to turn around the relationship. The husband was telling his father that he and his wife were on the verge of a divorce. The father asked him if he wanted to save the marriage, and the son admitted yes. So the dad gave his son a list of 40 activities and actions to do over the next 40 days, one for each day. The son wasn't happy about doing it, but he trusted his dad so he agreed.

The first morning, it was a simple task, "Put out a cup of coffee for your wife." The husband did, and felt a little positive from doing it. The wife came downstairs, took one look at the coffee, turned up her nose and stomped out of the house.

The next day, the husband got up early and made his wife's favorite breakfast and had it waiting on the table. And once again, when she saw what he had done, she turned up her nose and stomped out of the house.

This goes on for over a week, and every day it's the same negative response. The son finally phones his dad to complain and say this idea was dumb and that he quitting. The father admonished him gently and encouraged him to keep at it for the entire forty days.

"She doesn't believe you're sincere," the dad explained. "She thinks you're just putting on an act and you'll go back to your old hurtful ways. You have to show her you've changed."

So the son kept it up for forty days. Guess what happened? After a few weeks, the wife started to like the little things that her husband was doing. In fact, she also started to feel a little guilty. *He is being so nice to me,* she thought, *and I am treating him terribly in return. Maybe I need to change too.*

So here is the solution for 95% of relationship issues. It's really revolutionary. Ready? You decide to take personal responsibility for changing everything about yourself that bugs your partner, and do everything to make your partner happy that they've asked for and want. There you go! That will solve 95% of relationship issues.

A buddy of mine was considering a divorce. He had a young son. I asked him, "Years from now, do you want to be able to look your son in the eye and explain that you tried everything – everything humanly possible – to keep the marriage alive? Or do you want to say you gave up without even trying, knowing the pain that the breakup would cause him?"

My buddy answered immediately, "I want to be able to tell my son I did everything possible."

"Then," I replied, "You need to actually do everything possible to fix your marriage."

What else can you control? You could decide to read a dozen books on relationships and follow their advice. Completely clean up your own act. Here are some:

- The 5 Love Languages

- Crucial Conversations
- Seven Principles for Making Marriage Work
- His Needs, Her Needs

Obviously, sometimes the other person is the problem. There are real relationships that become abusive. You might be with a sociopath or someone whose mental health issues cause them to lash out at you. There are a few circumstances where leaving really is the best choice. But outside of those rarer circumstances, it's been my personal experience though that people more often than not choose to change their address rather than do the hard work of changing themselves.

My wife and I went through some serious relationship problems ourselves about ten years ago. I was mad at her, and she was mad at me. My mentor challenged me to look at my own heart and my own selfishness and begin to do the hard work of changing me.

I started reading every book I could find on marriage and relationships. And I decided that I was going to be a better husband. I knew that one thing my wife really liked was little notes that said lovely things. I started writing those notes all the time and leaving them on her pillow. Then, I decided to surprise her with red roses waiting on the dining table for when she came home. Then I started getting her red roses all the time, every couple of weeks. Then I upped the ante – I started picking up roses and bringing them to her office to leave on her desk. The first time I did this, her co-workers asked, "Is it your birthday? Your anniversary? Is he in trouble for something?" She explained that this was just what I do.

So my question to you is:

"What nice thing can you do today for the key relationships in your life?"

Even harder to consider: what nice thing can you do for someone who you're really ticked off at? That's a bigger accomplishment, don't you think? It's easy to do nice things for people we like. But I've discovered when I show kindness and thoughtfulness and caring towards someone I don't really like, it actually softens my heart towards them. Give it a try.

Finances

This is a major energy drain for many people. Again, doing yoga and deep breathing is great for managing stress, but when you're about to lose your house, those cute little balancing activities don't really cut it, do they? You need to use bigger firepower and tackle the actual problem.

The pandemic made many people's finances worse, but a lot of people had financial pressure before the pandemic. In 2017 Canadians had a debt-to-income ratio of 179%[1] (debt to income refers to how much debt someone has compared to how much after-tax income they have.) It seems that no matter how much money people make, they find a way to spend it.

Tackling this is as simple, and as uncomfortable as losing weight. Want to lose weight? It's really, really simple. The way you lose weight is you consume less calories than you burn. That means, for example, if you consume 2,900 calories in a day, you burn at least 3,000 calories. Simple – just not easy, particularly with so many delicious obstacles in your way, beckoning you with their siren song from the candy bar shelf in line at any store.

Managing your finances is also super simple: all you need to do is spend less than you make. Simple, right? Additionally, you might also choose to invest those savings wisely, and finally, you can increase your income-earning ability by increasing your skills and output. A very simple strategy, but also really difficult for a lot of people to follow. We make too many emotional choices: let's get a new fancy car, because we deserve it. Let's renovate our kitchen, because we deserve it. Let's buy the kids designer fashion clothes, and get them a Playstation 5, and shower them with toys... because they deserve it. Luxury vacation? You bet! We'll just put it on the Visa card.

I'm not a financial advisor, so I will simply point you in the direction of some resources that I have enjoyed. I think books like *The Richest Man in Babylon, Rich Dad Poor Dad,* and *The Wealthy Barber* all have some fantastic wisdom that is immediately applicable. Also, there are lots of wonderful apps and money-saving programs available for download. There is a veritable ocean of wisdom available online and at the bookstore.

Most people mistakenly believe that if they could increase their income, they could solve their money problems. I don't believe this to be true. I think no matter what income you are at, the income you imagine has someone else at that higher level and that person is making the same complaint about not having enough. If you have food, clothing, shelter, utilities, a computer with internet, cellphone, car, access to medicine, you are already wealthier than much of the planet. We need to change our mindset about what wealth constitutes.

The second mindset change is shifting what is a necessity versus a want. You might think a 70" TV is a necessity – but is it really? You don't have to purchase everything you want.

A third mindset to adopt is the idea of savings. Get really, really ruthless with paying yourself first, before you pay everyone else. If we don't prioritize savings, every penny gets swallowed up by those little bills and little purchases until we have nothing left.

Most people, if asked on the street, know what to do: track all of their expenditures – every penny. Write out a budget. Follow the budget. Stick to a savings plan. All of this sounds obvious – as obvious as following a diet to lose weight. Except in this case, most people need to go on a financial diet. Get a mentor, a trusted advisor, someone you can share your personal situation with and map out a plan of action. Most of our steps are emotional – meaning, we have to say "no" to some things today so that we can say "yes" to some more important and bigger things tomorrow. But if you follow through with a plan, it's amazing how you can reduce the financial pressure and headaches in your life that are draining you of money and of mental energy.

Career

A major energy drain for many people is their job. This can be a combination of many factors including workload, difficult clients, or not getting along with colleagues. The biggest factor of whether someone dislikes their job is their relationship with their boss. If you've got a fantastic boss whom you love working with, chances are you're going to enjoy your job a lot more. If you can't stand your boss, and they can't stand you, you're in for a world of hurt.

Imagine you've got the same workload, the same paycheque, but you have a lot of fun working with your colleagues, you enjoy each other tremendously, and you really like and respect your boss. Every time in their presence makes you feel happy, positive and energized. Just picturing that image can lift your spirits.

If you've got problems on your job, ask yourself what part of the problem you can fix. Maybe it's a process issue; a piece of software isn't working the way you need, or a process is frustration. Can you create an innovative solution to address the problem? Can you beta-test your solution, refine it, and present your findings to the entire team? Can you build goodwill around the idea and champion it so it has a greater chance of being adopted? I believe these things are more possible than many people estimate.

Maybe the role itself doesn't align with your talents. A powerful resource is the book *Now, Discover Your Strengths*. Take the time to really understand what you are good at, and see how that can be incorporated into your current role. There are a lot of well-intentioned motivational books that say you should follow your passion (which is a nice thought) and while doing so, you also need to pay your bills. Perhaps you could keep your current job and tack on an extra project that is more aligned to your passions, allowing you to safely grow into what you love. Why not create your dream job inside of the job you've already got?

A good question I like to ask is,

"If you won a hundred million dollars in the lottery, what would you work on for free for the joy of it?"

Most people, when they win the lottery, do some pretty standard things: they pay off debt, buy some toys like houses and cars, go on some amazing vacations, help their family and loved ones, give to charity, and enjoy some time sleeping in and lounging around. But after six weeks of binge-watching Netflix for 18 hours a day, you *might* start to get just a smidge tired of it and yearn for something more. So what would that be?

If you didn't have to work for money ever again – if you only worked for the pure joy of the task – what would you work on? Would you start a restaurant? Volunteer at an animal shelter? Go full-time into something creative like writing, art or film & media? Your answer to this would be very telling as to what your passions are. Once you clarify this, ask yourself, "How can I do some of what I love at my current job?"

I asked myself this question years ago. I was in sales, and what I really wanted to do was sales training and motivational speaking. Each week we would have a sales meeting, and I would volunteer to stand up and do a little ten-minute talk on sales. I loved doing it! I wasn't paid any extra money, but it was very fulfilling for me. I started to do more and more until opportunities became available to get paid to deliver training outside my own organization.

Finally, if you have a relationship problem at work, do your part to fix whatever you are contributing to the problem. Just as in resolving a marriage issue, you want to point the fingers back at yourself and ask:

"How could I change and help fix the situation?"

Some great books that have helped me with work relationships include *Speed of Trust, Crucial Accountability* and *Leadership & Self-Deception*.

It might seem easier to just quit and find a new job, and sometimes that is the correct answer. But I think you may find the same relationship problems creeping up in the new job, because you are still the same person. As my mentor Tim Marks says, "No matter where you go, there you are."

Become A Better You

In order to create a better life, we need to be a better person. The qualities of character that we exhibit are the foundation of our life experience. If we are passionate, we will have a passionate life. If we are excited, we will have an exciting life. If we feel blessed, we will have a blessed life.

Take a moment and consider the qualities of character that you wish to accentuate. Maybe you feel that you could be more confident, more charismatic, more diligent, more studied, more loyal, more supportive, better at listening, or better at showing compassion. Whatever the quality is, imagine that you could design a blueprint that showcases the ultimate version of your mind and personality. What would you like to strengthen in your personality? What qualities do you wish you had more of? As you identify these qualities, consider next what actions steps you could take in the next few days to exhibit the quality you desire.

Maybe you want to be more thoughtful, so you decide to pay attention when people are describing their family so that later you can ask about how they are doing. Perhaps you want to be more adventurous, so you decide to try out a new activity you've never done before. Maybe you want to increase the passion in your day, so you decide instead of giving your spouse a quick peck on the lips, you say farewell in the morning with a passionate 30-second kiss that makes your kids blush!

Have fun with this! Put a check mark next to each quality you would like to increase in yourself. I've suggested some examples of different qualities of character, but the potential list is much larger. I've left some room at the bottom for you to include your own examples. Then, decide what actions you can take in the next few days to exhibit these qualities!

What Can You Do Today To Be More...

- ❑ Thoughtful _____
- ❑ Adventurous _____
- ❑ Creative _____
- ❑ Passionate _____
- ❑ Confident _____
- ❑ Organized _____
- ❑ Grateful _____
- ❑ Appreciative _____
- ❑ Humble _____
- ❑ Spontaneous _____
- ❑ Relaxed _____
- ❑ Proactive _____
- ❑ Charismatic _____
- ❑ Diligent _____
- ❑ Compassionate _____
- ❑ Empathetic _____
- ❑ Supportive _____
- ❑ Loyal _____
- ❑ Intelligent _____

Now, I dare you to take action on one of these ideas before the day is done!

In conclusion, balance is more about finding the perfect strategy that works for you. Finding little moments through the day where you can pause and take a "joy break" to bring some happiness and light back into your life. It means saying "yes" to the things you love and making those things a priority in your life. Take time to take care of yourself, so that you can care for everyone you love. As S. McNutt says, "Fall in love with taking care of yourself. Fall in love with the path of deep healing. Fall in love with becoming the best version of yourself but with patience, with compassion and respect to your own journey."

CHAPTER 4: PHYSICAL ENERGY

"I am not an early bird or a night owl. I am some form of permanently exhausted pigeon." - Anonymous

PHYSICAL ENERGY

One of the hallmarks of burnout is physical exhaustion. No matter what other positive steps you feel you can or should take to recharge your batteries, nothing seems to move the needle when you are running on empty. When you are dragging yourself through your day and just trying to put a perfunctory "check mark" next to a few essential tasks, no other self-care strategy will provide as immediate a boost to your overall well-being than taking care of your body and overall energy level.

There are four key areas to manage your physical energy level. They are nutrition, hydration, sleep, and exercise. Let's get into each one.

Fueling Your Body with Nutrition

"Every time you eat or drink, you are either feeding disease or fighting it." – Heather Morgan

First on the "greatest hits list" of causes of physical exhaustion is poor nutrition. Now, let me say this is not going to be a big lecture on losing weight. In fact, truth be told, I put on ten pounds myself last summer through COVID. I typically am pretty regimented on my eating, but along with the rest of the planet I slipped back into eating some "comfort food" in the summer time. Just keeping it real.

So, this section is not about looking good for summer. What we are going to talk about is food as fuel: how it gives you energy, and how you can use it to manage your focus, mental health and vitality through the day. After all, don't you notice how it's hard to stay sharp and on your game when you are dragging yourself through the day? We've all had days like this. So, a big secret to keeping yourself in a good place through a year that is already draining is to make sure the good food we are eating is doing its job and putting fuel in our tank.

I know what I'm talking about here. I come from an exercise background. I am an award-winning competitive bodybuilder and have experience as a personal trainer. In a 90-day sprint I once packed on 27lbs of lean muscle mass. And I see a lot of people make some big mistakes with managing their diet.

First up: carbohydrates, or carbs, are **not your enemy**. In the correct amount, they are your best friend. They are a critical necessity from proper metabolic functioning. They are the fuel in your gas tank.

When you ingest carbohydrates, your body breaks the food down and coverts it into glucose; what is commonly referred to as "blood sugar." Your bloodstream absorbs the glucose and it is used by your cells for energy. This is really important to understand. If you are in a low-carb, low-sugar state, you are *going to feel tired*.

When I am getting ready for a body building competition and in the final "cutting" phase – which represents both cutting (reducing) carbs from my diet and looking "cut" or defined as a result – it's an exhausting experience. I am like a zombie walking around. My son could beat me in a wrestling match. It's not something you can keep up for long (nor should you – and definitely should only be attempted with expert supervision.) The point is this: when your blood sugar is low, you are in a low-energy state.

So, what do we tend to do when we get tired? Picture your office environment, pre-COVID. Our bodies have a circadian rhythm; the natural ebb and flow of hormones that regulate our sleep cycle. We experience a regular and predictable drop in these hormones around 3pm in the afternoon, and 3am in the morning. So, when the average office worker starts getting tired around 3pm, what do they reach for? For starters, they reach for caffeine, like a coffee. But what else do they reach for? Sugar – otherwise known as simple carbohydrates. And we have a bad habit of reaching for the bad-for-us sugars.

Back in the early 2000's, there was a lot of attention given to "low-carb, no-carb" diets. They seemed all the rage at the time, in no small part because they caused you to lose weight! Since weight loss seemed like a good goal, people flocked to these diets to replicate the results their friends were getting.

Why were these diets effective? That depends upon your definition of "effective." If you measure it in weight loss, I suppose they were effective. People would see the number on the scale drop and feel that the diet was working. The problem was that the scale doesn't differentiate between losing fat and losing lean muscle mass. You want to keep your lean muscle, and it becomes harder and harder to do as you age.

The low-carb diets were born because people noticed a very real behavioural problem: most people tend to over eat carbs. That includes junk food like soda pop, ice cream, pizza and chocolate. It also includes alcohol like beer and wine. Even "good" carbs are like candy for your body. Pasta, bread, butter – your mouth loves it and your body scoops it up. Think of your typical Thanksgiving or Christmas dinner table. You've got one plate of turkey, one plate of ham, perhaps a serving bowl of meatballs, and fourteen dishes of carbs. Bread, pasta, rice, mashed potatoes, all served with an extra wallop of gravy (carbs and fat) and butter (carbs and fat). These all taste great, so we keep eating them.

There are two main types of carbohydrates: simple, and complex.[li]

Simple Carbohydrates. These are a single molecule and can be metabolized very quickly, causing your blood sugar level to increase quickly. They provide an immediate boost of energy, but are not always the healthiest choice. Examples would be candy, fruit, soda pop, white bread, dessert cakes and pastries, donuts, pizza, jam, and honey.

Complex Carbohydrates. These are a longer chain of molecules, resulting in a longer time required to metabolize and enter the bloodstream. Examples would include whole grain bread and pasta, vegetables, legumes (such as peanuts) those rich in fiber such as broccoli, and those rich in starch such as brown rice.[lii]

Now, there are further factors to consider. For example, while fruit like apples contains fructose, a simple carbohydrate, its metabolic uptake is blunted by the fiber in the apple. This means you don't get the same "kick" that a candy bar filled with processed sugar would give you. Additionally, fruits such as apples contain essential nutrients, antioxidants, polyphenols, vitamins and minerals.[liii] So don't be scared of eating an apple. Personally, I love apples.

When you ingest a soda pop, your blood sugar gets jacked up pretty quickly. This is caused by the refined sugar (and the caffeine) in the soda pop. The result? You feel a reaction. You've got a little more bounce in your step. For a little while, you have some more energy. So you believe this is a good strategy to manage your energy, particularly at 3 pm when you're hitting that afternoon energy wall.

Then, something happens. In a short period of time (approximately twenty minutes) you start to really feel a depletion of energy. You almost feel more tired than you did before you had the soda pop. You want to turn this around quick, and you decide the best way to do this… is to have another soda pop! Right? Wrong.

What's happening is your body senses that your blood sugar levels have gone too high, too quickly. So, your pancreas secrets insulin to help bring your blood sugar level back to a normal level.[liv] If the sugar isn't used, the insulin helps place it into long-term energy storage and aids in converting it into something else: fat.[lv]

Long story short: start reducing (if not eliminating) the amount of simple carbohydrates in your diet – particularly processed sugars in junk foods and soda pop – and switch instead to using complex carbohydrates as your fuel source.

A table spoon of processed sugar will give you twenty minutes of energy. A banana gives you energy for two hours. It's a slower uptick and you don't feel the kick; you just notice that you're not quite as tired. The key is not to wait until your tired; have the banana half an hour before you expect to feel drowsy. That's a smart way to manage your energy.

Hydration – Your Body Needs Water

"Pure water is the world's first and foremost medicine." – Slovakian Proverb

Sometimes when we feel fatigue, what we are actually feeling is dehydration. You hear a lot about needing to drink water through the day, right? There is a reason.

Your body is approximately 60% water, and our blood is 90% water.[lvi] By the time your mouth starts to feel dry, you've already passed the point where you needed to be drinking. Severe dehydration can cause brain swelling, kidney failure and seizures.[lvii] Here are some more reasons why it's critical to stay hydrated:

- **Water boosts your energy level.** One study found that drinking 500 milliliters of water boosted metabolic rate in both men and women for an hour.[lviii]
- **Water helps regulate your mood**, decreasing tension and anxiety, and helping promote a greater feeling of calm.[lix]
- **Dehydration causes impairment in mental focus.** Since water accounts for 75% of brain mass, clinical studies have tracked how a decrease in water volume in your brain has a measurable impact on cognitive performance.[lx] Meaning, when you are thirsty, you aren't as sharp at work.
- **Water helps regulates body temperature** and keeps your body cool. In addition, water lost through sweat needs to be replenished in order to maintain proper hydration.[lxi]

There are a dozen other benefits, including how water aids in vitamin and mineral absorption, digestion of foods, and metabolic processes. Water is good for you!

Tips for drinking more water:

- **Keep a water bottle handy** or glass of water at your workspace. If it's in front of you, you are more likely to notice it and remember, "Hey, I should have some water!"
- **Set a reminder** on your watch and cellphone. Have it go off at regular intervals; perhaps once an hour works well as a reminder for you.
- **Sip regularly through the day.** You don't need to gulp back the whole bottle. Every once in a while, take a sip.
- **Use water flavoring.** These are great! My wife is a big advocate of these. I never used them before the pandemic and now I'm a fan. Your grocery store should have a wide variety to choose from. Experiment with a few to find a taste you like.
- **Use a water bottle with a fruit infuser**. Amazon carries these, and they great. If you haven't seen one before, look it up. There is a little plastic section in the middle of the bottle, with punch holes to allow water to flow freely through. You simply insert a slice of fruit of your choice, whether it's a slice of orange, lemon, or whatever is to your taste. Then, you've got fruit flavored water, and it has the benefit of being the real thing.

A final note: some people drink a lot of soda pop for the day and might not understand the health impact of water versus soda. Soda obviously does contain water, and if you were in a situation with no other water source available, you would absolutely benefit from drinking soda pop to stay hydrated.

However, most soda pop contains caffeine, a natural diuretic. Diuretics cause your kidneys to product urine – meaning you need to go to the bathroom more often.[lxii] High levels of caffeine can lead to dehydration. Additionally, the refined sugar in soda can spike your glucose levels. While soda pop is better than nothing, try to make a point of drinking pure, refreshing water. Your body will thank you for it.

Getting a Good Night's Sleep

"Go to bed and you'll feel better tomorrow" is the human version of "Did you try turning it on and off again?" – Unknown

Sleep is absolutely critical for your health, energy level and overall wellbeing. In fact, if we go 24 hours without sleep, our cognitive ability is so impaired that our reaction speed is reduced to the level of a drunk driver who blows over the legal alcohol limit.[lxiii] (Which, as a side note, is a really good reminder to never get behind the wheel when you're sleep deprived.) Sleep is a critical event each day where our body repairs itself, including rebuilding damaged cells, and on a cognitive level, sorting out the billions of bits of sensory data you are inundated with every day.

When you're run down and sleep deprived, you can feel that you're "off". You feel mentally sluggish, grumpy, irritable, your short- and long-term memory suffers, and performing simple cognitive tasks seems harder and invites more mistakes.[lxiv] Simply put, when we are sleep-deprived, we aren't performing at our best.

Today, many Canadians struggle with getting proper sleep. In a 2011 study, researchers at Université Laval found 40% of the two thousand people surveyed experienced at least three bouts of insomnia a week.[lxv]

Sleep problems were well-documented before the pandemic. But through the pandemic, the number of people experiencing sleep difficulties has skyrocketed. Three distinct sleep patterns have emerged: people getting less sleep due to stress and insomnia, people sleeping more as emotional and physical exhaustion take their toll, and people experiencing a shift in their schedules – meaning they stay up later and wake up later.[lxvi]

Our bodies have an internal clock that tells us when to wake up and when to go to bed. This cycle of wakeful energy level is your circadian rhythm. The National Institute of General Medical Sciences defines circadian rhythm as "the physical, mental, and behavioral changes that follow a 24-hour cycle. These natural processes respond primarily to light and dark and affect most living things, including animals, plants, and microbes."[lxvii] We generally refer to this as our "body clock". One factor that affects our body clock is the amount of light – it's a signal to our body that it's daytime, and we should be awake. But we also fall into a rhythm based upon our daily schedule. And the stress and altering of our normal daily schedules has thrown our biological rhythms right out of whack.[lxviii]

Struggling to get to sleep at the usual time, people start finding creative solutions. One solution people turn to is using a chemical depressant to help "knock themselves out." Alcohol would be one example of a depressant. Unwinding at the end of a stressful day with a well-deserved nightcap of brandy to help soothe the tension and drift off to dreamland. Sounds inviting, but it would be a mistake. Alcohol interrupts your dream state, otherwise known as REM or

Rapid Eye Movement. Your body might get rest through the night, but cognitively speaking, the next day your brain is still fuzzy.[lxix]

Additionally, taking a drug may help you drift off, but may not be a good idea. For example, some pills are allergy-symptom medications that have a side-effect of drowsiness the next day.[lxx] Others may target certain receptors in the brain that inhibit alertness.[lxxi] A melatonin supplement is often safer, because melatonin is the hormone your brain produces in response to darkness, signaling a relaxation response in preparation for sleep.[lxxii] However, be aware that if we start taking a melatonin supplement, it may send a signal to our brain to tell it to stop producing the correct level of melatonin. Additionally, with any supplement, we can become desensitized over time, requiring us to take more and more to feel the same original effect. So, check with your doctor and follow their advice.

While it's easy to turn to the quick-fix of a sleeping pill in the hopes of getting a more restful night in bed, there are some better and healthier options.

It's understandable that we would turn to these options, particularly if after a long hard day, finally climb into bed… only to stare at the ceiling, finally wide-awake and alert, annoyed that we aren't falling asleep, knowing that we've got to get up in six hours, knowing that we MUST be unconscious right now or tomorrow will be another day ruined by exhaustion. Sound familiar? I know I've struggled with that.

The first key is to create something called an **unwinding ritual**. For those of you with kids, this will be a familiar reminder. Remember back when they were babies (unless they are babies right now!) and you helped them get acclimated to this amazing thing called "life"? You probably created some routines to help them get a sense of the flow of their day. And, I'll bet one of those routines was a bedtime routine.

For our son, we would feed him dinner… and at least some of it would go in his mouth. The rest of it he would either end up wearing on his face or clothing, or he would use it (despite our best efforts) to colorfully decorate his highchair. Then, off to the bathtub! We would scrub him clean, and get him into his little jammies. The lights would be turned down, and we might give him a final nighttime bottle, before laying him in his crib. As he got older, we would start to read stories. But the main point of this was that there were a series of cues to let him know that we were winding down for bed.

As adults, we benefit greatly from the same sort of habitual structure. Since we've been moving at light-speed all day, we need a way of telling ourselves that it's time to take our foot off of the gas pedal and calm down. Certain events or actions, repeated over and over, let our brains know that "Hey! It's time to wind down!" And we start calming ourselves and slow ourselves down to prepare for sleep.

I'm going to recommend you experiment with a regular unwinding ritual. You want to aim for soothing, calming activities. Here are some things to avoid right before bed:

- Eating or drinking anything with caffeine (unless you need to safely drive home and you would benefit from a little coffee. Safety is always the priority.)
- Avoid watching any action or intense horror movies. Aside from the fact that they startle you into alertness, your subconscious chews on whatever you are intensely focused on right before sleep, and right when you wake up. You've probably noticed this if the alarm clock goes off and the radio plays a song – even if it's a song you find annoying. All of a sudden,

you've got that song stuck in your head all day. The same is true just as you are falling asleep. Try to focus on relaxing, pleasant things.

- Getting into a massive fight with a loved one. I've read a lot of books that say, "Don't go to bed angry. Stay up and work it out." Well, I believe the spirit of that is that you should both agree to resolve the issue, rather than avoid it, and you should both reaffirm your love for each other, and forgive each other, rather than heading to bed in a foul mood. I personally don't think it's generally a good idea to work through big important relationship issues at 4 am when you are exhausted and more likely to blurt out something hurtful that you regret saying. Kiss and makeup, get some sleep, and tackle it in the morning.
- Minimize the "blue light" from screens, or even better, stop watching screens entirely. Blue light interrupts melatonin production, the hormone responsible for helping you get to sleep.

So, what are some great unwinding actions you can take?

- Have a nice warm bath. I find a shower before bed refreshing, and my wife loves a hot bath.
- Drink some chamomile tea. Many people have discovered they find this to be a relaxing experience, and the tea itself promotes a better night's sleep.[lxxiii]
- Personally, I enjoy playing some light piano before bed. For me, it's relaxing. My wife (who loves to paint) will often do some basic paint-by-numbers; it doesn't require any thinking, there is no chance to get upset, and she finds it calming.

- Deep breathing and meditation are fantastic unwinding exercises.
- I love to read right before bed. In fact, I find I often suffer from "reading narcolepsy." I started nodding off, my head hits the book, and I know it's time to turn off the light.
- And finally, my new favorite unwinding habit: I say "goodnight" to my Google Home Nest, and I have programmed it to play a narration that walks through deep breathing exercises and has gentle wind chimes. It shuts itself off after thirty minutes, and I have already drifted off. I love it. (Seriously, if you don't have one of these gadgets, it's really worth considering.)

Once you've got that main strategy down, what else can we do to improve sleep? Make your bedroom as comforting and relaxing as possible. Here are some tips how:

- Reduce noise. Either use foam earplugs, or a white noise generator. What's that? Basically, it's a fan whose noise covers up outside noises, such as a car driving by or a door closing. The fan is loud enough that you only hear it. The benefit is that any sensory data our brain receives that is constant is something we will quickly start to ignore. This reduces cognitive congestion and lets your brain focus on more important things. You've experienced this before if you notice something new on the wall. Initially, we notice everything new to determine if it's a threat or a benefit. Once we've answered that, and it stops moving and the novelty has worn off, we start to ignore it completely. It becomes like wallpaper to us.

The same thing happens with a fan or a white noise generator. A word of caution though: if you are using a standard fan, make sure it doesn't oscillate. The motion of it rotating back and forth will change the sound you hear, keeping you aware of it and potentially interrupting sleep.
- Keep your room and the bed sheets and pillowcase cool. Our bodies actually prefer a slightly cooler temperature at night. So, if you can program your thermostat to drop a degree or two (not ten!) then do so. Experiment with what feels good for you. I actually keep two pillows for this reason: when one becomes warm, I switch to the cooler one and it feels great.
- Invest in your mattress! Seriously: how old is your mattress? Was it purchased this decade? A Christmas gift from my wife this year was a wonderful new mattress. There are a lot of great ones to choose from. But consider this: at 6 hours a day, 25% of your entire life is spent on you mattress. At 8 hours a day, that jumps to 33% of your life spent on your mattress. Since getting a quality night's sleep has so much power over your mood and cognitive ability the next day, doesn't this seem important? If you're still not convinced, how about this gross fact: guess what lives in your mattress? Little tiny critters. Guess what they feed on? The dead skin cells that you shed all day long. (BTW, most of the dust in your home is actually just your skin.) You can try vacuuming the mattress, but why not serve these little monsters a permanent eviction notice and get a new mattress. Pronto.
- **Put on new sheets.** It feels great to slip into clean, fresh sheets. Throw on a fresh pair. And, maybe

splurge and treat yourself to some 800 thread count sheets, or satin. Slip into a luxurious experience!

- **Leave the electronics in another room.** Just don't bring your iPad or cellphone to bed. It's killing your sleep. One text or email comes in, or something pops up on Facebook, and it wakes you out of your slumber when you should be calming down your mind. Best advice? Turn it off and plug it in to charge downstairs in your kitchen. The further away from you it is, the better rest you're going to get. And I know you just love to watch Netflix on your iPad in bed. Do it in another room. Do it in the family room or entertainment room. It trains your brain to get triggered by your environment that the other room is for screens, and the bedroom is for sleep. Seriously, I keep my bedroom looking like a monastery. I treasure getting a good night's sleep.

Here's the final point, as we conclude our talk on sleep. Consider what morning of the week feels the worst to wake up for most people. Monday morning, right? That's a pretty consistent experience for many people. Now, consider that most people stay up a little later on Friday and Saturday night socializing and having fun, and then sleep in Saturday and Sunday morning to get some extra rest. They've "earned" sleeping in because they worked hard all week. Now, what does staying up late and sleeping in do to your sleep schedule? It pushes it back an hour or two. Then you get up again Monday morning on your normal workday schedule and feel especially groggy, because 6am now feels like 5am or 4am. And repeat this pattern every weekend, year after year, for decades. No wonder we feel yucky on Monday mornings! (Also, a major factor to feeling yucky on Monday morning's is the person is going back to face the stress that waits at the office. We're just focusing on physiology at the moment.)

Here is the #1 tip I can give you to manage the quality of your sleep… and you're not going to like it. Heck, I don't even like it. But it sure does work.

Try to go to bed at the same time every night, but most especially, make sure to get *up* at the same time every day of the week… including Saturday's and Sunday's.

Horrible idea, right? But if you would actually bite the bullet and just do this for two or three weeks in a row, you'd start to notice something really interesting. Your sleep cycle would become more regulated, and you wouldn't be as fatigued at the beginning of the week. Your eyes would actually start opening up a few minutes before the alarm went off. And your overall energy level would start to increase. The more consistently you did this, you'd notice the better you feel overall.

Now the first Saturday morning you do this, you are going to be ticked off that you are putting yourself though this. You'll grumble and complain and want to hit the snooze button. Don't do it. You're facing the same physical grogginess that you face Monday's, except without having to endure the additional psychological baggage of dealing with work stress. It's just your body that's tired. So fight through that first weekend. If you do this as an experiment for two or three weeks, you'll notice a difference in your energy level, and you'll probably sell yourself on the idea of keeping up this habit forever.

I Know I Should Exercise, I Just Don't Want To

"If you don't make time for exercise, you'll probably have to make time for illness." – Robin Sharma

As a former personal trainer, I marveled at how we would make half of our annual gym membership sales in the first three weeks of January. Everyone was fired up about their New Year's Resolution goals, (which is great) and they'd hit the gym with renewed motivation (which is great.) The gym would be incredibly crowded (which was not pleasant) and people would be waiting for a machine to open up to use. Then, miraculously, by about the third week of January, those big crowds would start to fade away, because people would lose motivation on their fitness goals.

Not great.

So, do you have a "friend" who has gone through a similar experience as this? Maybe, someone you know intimately? Perhaps, someone you see in the mirror every day? If so, I've got great news. I'm here to help you solve this, once-and-for-all.

Ask yourself, "What's the #1 most common reason people tell themselves (and tell everyone else) why they didn't exercise that day?" Think about it for a minute. Here's the one I've heard hundreds of times:

"I didn't have enough *time*."

That is the #1 excuse I hear. That is followed closely by "I was too tired" or "I didn't want to/I lack motivation." These are getting closer to the truth.

Folks, I get it. I've been there. I have had days where I was so exhausted I could barely make it through the day. One day a few weeks back, I was so tired I laid down in bed at 10pm and slept almost until 7 am – 9 hours in total – which is very unusual for me. And on that day, I missed my workout. Nobody is perfect.

First of all, can we agree to the value of exercise for your overall health and wellbeing, let alone your overall energy? I'm not going to take any page space here to debate this: if you aren't sold on this already, go online and spend the afternoon researching it. One in five Canadian deaths each year is cause by heart disease and stroke.[lxxiv] It is the 2nd leading cause of death in Canada.[lxxv] The principle contributor to heart disease is poor lifestyle choices: poor nutrition and poor exercise habits. I encourage you to be sold on this.

Now, we might intellectually understand something to be true, and yet still munch away on our potato chips and spend the day on the couch surfing Netflix. That's reality; I get it. So the first step is saying, "CJ, I realize exercise would be good for me. How do I get myself to do it?" That's a great place to start.

First up: the time excuse. This is a prioritization issue, not a lack of time. Meaning, we tend to find time for things we really want to do. What makes us want to do something? If there is a massive immediate reward, or a massive immediate consequence. So, here's a simple mental exercise: If I offered you one million dollars cash if you would do sixty seconds of any exercise of your choice – pushups, jumping jacks, stair climb, planks, jogging outside, exercise cycle, treadmill – would you do it? Could you carve out sixty seconds from your busy schedule by midnight tonight to do the exercise? You bet you would! It's rhetorical. Everyone would.

Now, flip side: what if I told you that you were going to die if you didn't start doing exercise… would you do it then? You've probably heard stories of people who had serious heart conditions. I knew a guy had let his health and diet deteriorate for years and had put on over 100 pounds of extra weight. After years of neglecting his health he finally landed in the hospital. His heart had an 80% blockage in one artery and his heart was swollen to 150% it's normal size. They needed to inject dye into his heart to see a clear image of the blockage on a special monitor, and injecting the dye might kill him. He was in bad shape. Do you think this guy, potentially laying on his death bed, resolved in his mind, "If I survive this, swear I am going to cut out the beer, the red meat, and start working out again?" You bet.

It shouldn't take a life-threatening wake-up call for us to make a change and jar us out of complacency, but sadly it often does require that. Sometimes people learn the lesson in time to make a change. Sometimes, it's too late for them.

So what can we do to get ourselves to exercise?

First, take baby steps. I'd hear clients say, "I'm going to work out three hours a day, seven days a week, until I lose this weight!" No; no you won't. Let's be serious. You'll just quit that and have another reference point of making a big claim and then not following through. That's not better for you.

Instead of a three-hour marathon, all I want you to do is form a baby-step habit. A daily habit that becomes part of your identity: "I am someone who exercises daily." Keep it really simple and really small. So, what is an amount of time that you feel is reasonable that you can do every single day, no matter what? Maybe it's 20 minutes. Perhaps 10 minutes. Maybe it's just one minute. That's fine, because it's a starting point.

Just commit every day you're going to do one minute of exercise, and build up from there. I would be proud of anyone for doing an hour of exercise once. I would be very, very impressed if you did one minute, every day, for a month. Now you're building a habit, and that's much more powerful long-term. (As an extra resource on this topic, James Clear has written an entire book titled *Atomic Habits* that I couldn't more highly recommend.)

Make the baby step so small, it seems ridiculous not to do it. Suppose you resolve that you will literally just go to your basement, and sit on your exercise bike, and turn the pedals one time. Once. It would take you one second. Then, what would happen is your brain would say, "This is silly. I am already here. I can probably pedal the bike for thirty seconds." Now we're talking! Now you've overcome inertia and you have a starting to get yourself to take a positive step forward. Trick yourself into beginning by doing a super-tiny baby step.

Now, let's decide what the exact activity will be. Specificity in your goal is powerful. It gives you a clear image of what you're trying to accomplish, so there is a clear finish line to say "I've accomplished my task." With picking an exercise activity, particularly during this pandemic having many public gyms closed for the time being, look at what you can you do at or around your home with the equipment you have available.

You don't need to spend a lot of money for equipment. In fact, you don't need to spend any – there are a lot of bodyweight exercises you can do with zero equipment. But take stock. What do you have around your house right now?

- ❏ Exercise bike/treadmill/elliptical
- ❏ Dumbbells
- ❏ Bicycle

❑ Skipping rope
❑ Running shoes for jogging
❑ Other: _____

A lot of people flocked to stores like Fitness Depot as the lockdown wore on to get some equipment, which is great. I felt glad that I had invested over the years in gym equipment. I buy everything used on Kijiji and get it for crazy low prices. I've got a universal with attached leg press, an Olympic free weight bench press, battle ropes, punching bag, multiple dumbbells, and an exercise bike. In time I will get some other toys that I have my eyes on. I like this stuff because part of my identity is that I work out and stay in shape. The other part is massive convenience: I never, ever, have to expend the effort and time to drive out to a gym. In fact, many times I will do 10 seconds of exercise just as I am walking through my basement. I might bring a load of laundry down, and as I am waiting 20 seconds for the laundry machine to fill up with water, I might fire off a set of bench press or pulldowns or battleropes. When you make things really easy and simple for you to do, you are more likely to do them.

Let's suppose you have no equipment at all. It's time for bodyweight exercises! There are a bunch to enjoy. They include:

❑ Push ups
❑ Jumping jacks
❑ Sit ups or crunches
❑ Planks
❑ Isometric wall sit
❑ Assisted squats
❑ Glute bridges
❑ Dead bugs (watch these online)

- ❏ Stair climbs (assuming you have stairs)
- ❏ Going for a hike
- ❏ Jogging outside
- ❏ Dancing! (See? Why not have some fun?)

Here's a great thing to do: watch some exercise programs online. Our basement is half home-entertainment for the boys, half gym. I love to have the big screen playing YouTube exercise videos, some of which are motivational with music, and some of which are instructional. I also own an old DVD set of an exercise program called P90X. This may not be to your taste, but I really like it. You can also find a bunch of fitness cardio trainers with YouTube channels that not only explain exercises, but take you through a whole timed 20-minute class. There are hundreds to choose from. (For those of you who love bodybuilding fitness, I am a big fan of Athlean-X, but I also realize this is not to everyone's taste.)

So, once you've picked your activity, now it's time to decide when and where you're going to do it. Chip and Dan Heath, authors of *Switch*, describe this as an "action trigger".[lxxvi] You have a measurably higher chance of following through on an action when you clearly decide in advance where and when you are going to do it. So, you might say, "Each day at 4pm I am going to go to the rec room, get on my exercise bike, and ride for 5 minutes." That's very specific and exactly the way I recommend you picture doing your activity.

Next up: tell as many people as possible. Sounds a little scary? Just go for it! Get onto Facebook and announce to the world, "Hey friends and family! I've decided that I want to make a positive change in my health. And so, each day at 4pm, I am going to ride my bike for 5 minutes." Now we're talking! If you want to add a little extra positive motivation, let people know you will text them a picture of the bike as you are riding it. If you're anything like me, I feel more motivated to follow through on things when I know I'm accountable to people I love, and when I have a big audience watching. Maybe it's just my personality, and maybe it's part of being a human being. But I think we all want to put our best foot forward when we know we are in the spotlight.

A word of caution: this is not meant to stress you out. It's meant to put a little positive pressure on yourself to follow through on a good habit. It's worked many times for me and so I continue to use this tool. Give it a try and see if it works for you. If not, no worries! This book is meant to bring you peace, not leave you wound up and stressed over a self-imposed pressure. However, here's what else I have found: once you get rolling, the positive energy and positive response will really make you feel great. In fact, when you announce your fitness goal to the world (even a tiny goal) you may notice that your Facebook is flooded with wonderful support from friends and family cheering you on. That's a great feeling.

Once you get on a roll, you may find it becomes a positive addiction. I love exercising, even when I don't feel like doing it. Once I get through a few sets, my heart is pumping, I am alert, and I feel good. That good feeling carries you through a lot of the day. Because of that, it's become a major part of my life. And, I've found a secret formula to make sure it happens like clockwork. The secret formula is my morning power routine.

My Morning Power Routine

"When you arise in the morning, think of what a precious gift it is to be alive – to breathe, to think, to enjoy, to love." – Marcus Aurelius

For myself, I find that starting and ending my day with a ritual is a very empowering experience. Prior to the pandemic, I would do this robotically at 6am. Through the pandemic, like many people I've also eased up on some things and allowed myself a little flexibility. I will sometimes do this at 6:30 or 7 am, or sometimes at 8am when our son heads out the door to school (it's back and forth right now – a child in his class just had COVID last week, and we were back to homeschooling for him again for 14 days.) My pre-COVID regimented schedule has taken a back-seat to easing up some pressure on myself. I'm following some of my own advice here!

Each morning, my alarm goes off, and it's become one of my favorite experiences of the day. Last summer in the middle of the pandemic lockdown, I purchased a Google Home Nest for my bedside table, and I love it. I say "good morning" and it begins playing some symphony music I've selected that starts softly and increases in vigor, shifting to soundtrack action-music. Then, it calls up motivational talks that cycle between some of my favorite speakers including Tony Robbins and Les Brown. I enjoy this for a few minutes and then swing my feet out of bed.

When my feet hit the carpet, I make the bed, walk into the hallway, drop to my knees, and do ten pushups. With rare exception, it's every single morning nearly 365 days a year.

There are three key reasons I do pushups as soon as I get out of bed:

1. **It destroys the time excuse.** Most people complain that they don't have time to exercise. You annihilate this mental excuse when you break the action down to a bite-sized baby step. It only takes ten seconds, and everyone has ten seconds. Why stop at ten, and not twenty or fifty or one hundred? Because it's not strenuous, it's quick and simple – making it really easy to execute, and more likely I won't back out.

2. It gives **a boost of oxygenated blood** to my brain, helping me shake off the proverbial cobwebs. It gets my heart pumping just a little bit as I start my day.

3. It helps me **start the day with a victory**. So much of our lives, especially during the pandemic, people feel like they are out of control. The antidote is to do what you can control. And, you can control doing ten pushups. Additionally, you showed a little burst of discipline and self-control, pushing yourself to do a little task that most people would never push themselves to do. That's worthy of feeling a little proud. Imagine that you began every day of your life, and your first action was to do something that made you proud of yourself. Don't you think that would have a positive upward compound effect on your day? You bet it would.

Another point: a lot of our daily actions are done on basic autopilot. Studies suggest over 40% of our actions are habit-based.[lxxvii] So, use this to your advantage: create positive habits that you do without thinking. With the pushups, I do it in the exact same spot in my hallway, every morning. (It is so specific that when I would travel – pre-COVID – and be in any other city or hotel, the different room would throw me off my game and sometimes I would forget to do the pushups immediately.)

Once I did my pushups, I'd head to the bathroom. I've got my goals on the wall in the bathroom and on the wall beside my bed, so I see them the minute I wake up. I would stand on the scale and snap a photo of my weight and send it to my bodybuilding coach.

Next up: I head downstairs to the fridge. I like to pre-make my food for a couple of days in advance so that I can just reach into the food and grab my next meal. (Special shout-out to my beautiful bride; through the pandemic, she has taken it upon herself to make a lot of those meals for me – call it an expression of love from her to me.) To start my day, I have pre-made my own special blend of veggie juice that I put into single-serving juice containers.

If you have not discovered homemade veggie juice, let me pause the conversation here: it ROCKS. A few years back, my wife bought a juicer for a diet she was on, and it quickly got appropriated by me. Tony Robbins wrote, "If you don't have a juicer, buy one. If you don't have the money, sell your car and get a juicer."

I've experimented with a bunch of different blends and found one that I really like. It's simple, easily replicated, and tastes great to me. I use:

- 2 apples
- ½ cucumber
- 4 carrots
- A slice of ginger

This concoction, especially served cold, tastes delicious. It gives me a great boost of healthy carbs as I start my day. And, since we are dehydrated when we wake from having fasted for 6-8 hours while sleeping, you want to get some water (or veggie juice) into your system as quick as you can when you wake up.

My final step for my power morning routine is exercise. I head down to my basement gym. Over the years I've invested in a lot into gym equipment for my basement – but you don't need to do that. You can do a lot of bodyweight exercises, and that won't cost you any money.

(As an aside, if you do buy gym equipment, always buy it used and on sale. I bought almost everything off of Kijiji and saved thousands. Someone else buys a treadmill for $2,000, never uses it, and posts it on Kijiji for pennies on the dollar. Seriously – buy used equipment.)

I will exercise for about 30 minutes in the morning. I do a split program where I work out my chest, shoulders and triceps on odd-calendar days, and I work out my legs, back and bicep on even-calendar days. I started doing this as a way of preventing the common habit of skipping leg day, and it's worked great for years.

There have been days where I am dog tired or in a rush out the door. In those days, I may do 5 minutes of weights. In fact, there have been a couple of days I am in such a rush, I literally have one minute to do a set of bench press or a set of leg press – and that's it. Guess what? I still do it, because it makes me feel great. Even if I am running low on energy, I long ago resolved that a crappy workout, where I was putting in half-effort, was always better than no effort. If for no other reason, it meant I was keeping up the habit, and I was at least exercising mental discipline. Some days, that's the victory. I also may choose to do a lighter workout on the days that I am feeling sick or run down, because working out (the way I do it) is deliberating and really breaks down your body. Occasionally, it makes sense to do a lighter workout.

In conclusion, with so much of burnout attributed to physical exhaustion, it seems on the surface that the obvious starting point is to take care of your body. You probably already know – and agree – that all these ideas would benefit you. Yet like many people you often find yourself zonked out on the couch at the end of the day – and you don't have a shred of juice to even make dinner. I get it. I've had days like that myself. You're going to have many more of those moments, and that's okay. Here's what you do in that moment: just do a tiny little step forward. It is just amazing how one baby step can inspire us to take another. You might be dog-tired, totally unable to do your usual thirty-minute cardio routine. Can you do ten jumping jacks? Can you reach for an apple instead of a candy bar? Can you reach for a glass of water rather than a Coke? Just a baby step is all I ask for tonight. Because you'll find, as I have, that doing it gives you a little glimmer of pride – you honored your commitment to yourself to bring a renewing habit into your day. Despite the dizzying avalanche of stuff we've faced this year, you still get to care for yourself.

Chapter 5: Virtual Fatigue

"I just survived another Zoom meeting that could have been an email." – Anonymous office worker

Prior to the pandemic, two problematic facets of our work experience were already spreading their tentacles into everyone's daily schedule: lots of time in meetings, and lots of time staring at our computer screens. Patrick Lencioni's book *Death By Meeting* already highlighted the first problem, making obvious that we were spending too much time in meetings, and part of the culprit was the way they were being run. The second problem, staring at your screen all day, seemed a necessary evil. How else to conduct modern business but through your computer? Every additional technological advance and contrivance, including teleconferences and eventually web conferences, would be readily adopted and rolled out to a technology-fatigued workforce.

Before the pandemic, however, these two things seemed to offer a bit of a buffer to the other. In many meetings, people would choose to look at people rather than their screen (though not always.) This would give your eyes and brain a break from too much "screen time" – the bane of parents everywhere. However, the lumbering inefficiency of most meetings was obvious, leading corporate titans like Jeff Bezos banning PowerPoint in favor of printed executive summaries that everyone read in silence, and Elon Musk insisting that people politely excuse themselves once they were no longer contributing or getting value. Staring at your screen certainly was efficient – but your brain needs a break through the day, and the valuable lubricant of human interaction to make your day smoother and more enjoyable. Meetings give you a chance to bond, connect and network, let alone share ideas and brainstorm collaboratively. Alone at your desk, we miss out on human connection.

With the onset of the pandemic, something really interesting happened: we lost both of those things. First, instead of spending four hours a day staring at your screen, and four hours a day in meetings, now you were spending all day long staring at your screen. The screen version of a meeting lost impact because much of the collaborative and social interaction, those human touch points, was now shrouded behind the technology.

It seemed after a while we found ourselves growing numb staring at the screen, all day long, and found ourselves in many, many more screen-facing meetings. And if humans are great at inventing positive things to lift ourselves up, we are just as clever and creative with inventing new ways to drive ourselves right into the ground. And so, in the middle of a virus ravaging our world, widespread economic crisis and global stress levels at an all-time high, we also managed to invent a whole-new form of fatigue: virtual fatigue.

Fortunately, once people were done sitting in their office chair staring at their laptop for Zoom meetings and writing reports, they turned to an obvious and popular strategy to decompress after a day of staring at work screens: they sat in their lounge chair watching Netflix, YouTube and TV.

If you've started to feel virtual fatigue, you're not alone. The world's most popular video conferencing platform, Zoom, saw an increase of 10 million users a month in February 2020 to over 300 million users by April 2020.[lxxviii] (Right now, I wish I had bought stock in Zoom. Anyone else feel this way?) And with this sudden massive increase in usage, we saw a commensurate increase in fatigue. "Zoom fatigue" became a popular term to describe what people were facing. (Of course, it's worth considering perhaps part of Zoom fatigue is that we're a year into a pandemic?) In his February 2021 article *Nonverbal Overload: A Theoretical Argument for the Causes of Zoom Fatigue*, author and researcher Jeremy N. Bailenson posits that there are four main reasons why people feel so drained after spending all day in virtual meetings.[lxxix] They are:

1. Eye Gaze at a Close Distance
2. Cognitive Load
3. An All-Day Mirror
4. Reduced Mobility

Let's dig into each one!

Eye Gaze At Close Distance

Consider the space around you when you are talking. In Western culture, we feel pretty comfortable when strangers are several feet away – the distance of our outstretched hand being able to reach their outstretched hand. With our intimate relationships, we get close enough for a hug or a kiss. Now picture the size of the person's head in your field of view when they are your spouse or child – pretty close, right? Now, all your colleagues on Zoom suddenly appear as close as our loved ones. Their faces now loom large in our field of view and our brain gets conflicting messages. Suddenly Alex from accounting is as close as my spouse and kids, and I'm not really sure I love Alex from accounting that much.

Picture stepping onto a crowded elevator and you keep your back to the door. Everyone stares directly at you, including the people who are 18 inches away, and now they are desperately trying to find their shoes interesting – anything to avoid having to interact with you or even acknowledge your existence. An elevator of people staring right at you would be unusual and simply feel weird. And "elevator awkwardness" is just part of normal Western culture. What if your personality temperament is more introverted and you feel social interaction to be draining. Now you are up-close and personal all day long on Zoom meetings.

The next problem you see with all the big faces on the screen is they are staring, wide-eyed, right at you. Even if you're not the speaker, you are suddenly on stage, being watched.[lxxx] I can tell you from experience as a professional speaker that this requires more energy because now you are "on" – you are performing for the audience. You want to look and act sharp, professional, engaged. You feel like you're being scrutinized and now you're hyper aware of everything. Am I smiling and nodding enough to seem engaged? Is my hair done right? Am I wearing the right clothes? Does the room look professional?

Professional speakers experience this heightened pressure to be "on" when they are onstage, even when they aren't speaking. Everyone is closely watching them. Even if I am seated on stage behind a table, participating on a panel and I don't have the microphone, I still have heightened awareness that I am being watched closely by everyone in the audience. Similarly, if I am sitting in a conference room waiting to go on stage and I am at the head table along with the leaders in the room, I am aware that I am in full public view, and, as a new face in the room and the likely keynote speaker, I am hyper-aware that I am being watched. Filling a glass of water is now more emotionally draining. This puts extra strain on you to be "on" and appear engaged. You might be answering a family member's off-screen question, or staring down at your notepad as you take notes. But you feel a pressure to apologize and explain yourself, describing what the off-camera interruption is. In a real-life scenario, the speaker would see it's just you writing. On a Zoom? Maybe they think you are just rude. So you fret that you're being misinterpreted as rude and unengaged.

Cognitive Load

Since so much communication is non-verbal, including body language cues, when we are on a Zoom a lot of that information is lost to us. We can't see if a person is fidgety because they are bored, or tell as easily if they want to interject and add a point, or are shifting uncomfortably because they don't understand. Because we lose a lot of this, it takes so much more effort to communicate over Zoom than when we are in person.

One factor suggested is how even a few-millisecond lag time between the video image of someone speaking and their words can be cognitively draining as your brain sorts out the discrepancy.[lxxxi]

We risk misunderstanding cues. If someone gets an email notification pop-up on their screen, they will probably glance to the left to check it out. However, onscreen, it looks like they are looking at someone or something else, which can cause a second of mild confusion. Your brain isn't used to getting these mixed messages.

For me, I miss the energy from a live audience. I like to be in the room with them and be able to see them smile, chuckle, perk up, and engage me. I can tell if I've got the room or if I am losing it. So it takes way more energy to present over the phone and over Zoom than in person. Presenting on Zoom is like talking into a void. To even be able to see someone nod in agreement, smile or laugh at a joke, or even furrow their brow in puzzlement – all of these things give me real-time cues as to how to shape my delivery. But without these cues? I'm shooting in the dark. I am guessing if my delivery is landing, and have to consciously manage my own self-talk that my audience that day is probably really engaged, enjoying this presentation and getting value. I have personally experienced much more enjoyment, and much less stress and energy drain, when I can see people's faces during the presentation.

It can also be distracting to deal with all the cute virtual backgrounds – one person is sitting on a tropical beach, one person is outside the Eiffel Tower on a fall day, one person is in a gilded cottage with a roaring fireplace in the background. And everyone has a choppy outline as the Zoom artificial intelligence does its best on the fly to cut out your background, leaving the edges of your hair a jagged computerized mess. If that isn't distracting enough, how about the people who forget to mute – so you get to hear all their household background noise, the dings and alerts coming through their computer when a message arrives, and their own career-limiting musings about "how long is this VP going to drone on?" They forgot they were talking with their unmuted "outside" voice. (Those comments might add some levity for the co-workers who dislike this person's continued employment.)

We also get tired sending exaggerated cues. We give a BIG smile and a BIG nod to compensate for not being present in the room. These actions require a little more effort and energy. It's like having to speak extra-loud to an ailing grandparent at the dinner table. They mean well, but a lot of the subtle nuance is lost when you are reduced to shouting the punch line of a story.

It's also stressful for "non-techies" to deal with all the buttons, features, inevitable glitches and hiccups that occur with any use of technology. I watched Tony Robbins deliver a 5-day online seminar with a virtual audience; his team highlighted one person that Tony began to interview and the audience member started talking, but with his microphone off. Tony's impregnable smile wavered just a little as he gently asked the person *several* times to please unmute – all with 700,000 people watching online. Tech glitches happen to all of us, and they can be stress-inducing.

Silence is another problem. On a Zoom when people go silent, you get worried that they aren't listening or have lost the signal. You worry that the connection is down or that you've done something wrong and accidentally muted yourself or logged off. This concern over technical issues creates additional stress, which is draining.[lxxxii]

An All-Day Mirror

Imagine in the physical workplace, for the entirety of an 8-hr workday, an assistant followed you around with a handheld mirror, and for every single task you did and every conversation you had, they made sure you could see your own face in that mirror. This sounds ridiculous, but in essence this is what happens on Zoom calls. All day long, there is a big mirror in your face, highlighting all your flaws. Every pimple, blemish, unplucked eyebrow hair, unkempt hairdo, messy attire, or facial twitch is magnified when a big camera is staring at you and you're watching your image on the screen.

And most people when watching a Zoom don't stare directly into the camera, which would allow them to seem to be making direct eye contact – it appears that they are staring slightly off to the side, because they are looking down at the faces on the screen. And, guess whose face most people are looking at most of the time? You guessed it – themselves. We are so egocentric that whenever a picture or video of us pops up, we are pulled like a moth to the flame and just need to stare are our favorite subject. Don't believe me? Next time you look at a family photo filled with a dozen aunts and uncles and cousins, just pay attention to who you look at first. Who do you think most people look at first? Themselves! We find ourselves endlessly fascinating.

Environment-Conscious

At work, you can get yourself all gussied-up and looking sharp. Zoom call at home? Now everyone in your office is staring at your dirty laundry – both real and proverbial.

Initially, before we set up her new office space in the master bedroom, my wife would do Zoom meetings from our son's room. Some of you have had this experience I am sure. Her meeting attendees were graced with typical 13-year-old boy posters and decorations, adding some colorful "humor" to her meeting. She would laugh it off, explain it away and move on, but it always seemed a bit silly to her and distracting from the seriousness of the calls she would be on.

During the pandemic, one of our two cats needed surgery. Afterwards, the cat was in a purple onesie to keep it from licking the surgery stiches on her belly and causing infection. This cat, Millers, either appropriates my wife's office chair or sits in her lap during meetings. During one particularly eventful meeting, as my wife was discussing an important initiative, her staff watched a cat head slowly emerge from her lap, standing upward into the frame, adorned with the purple onesie. The staff couldn't help themselves, and one employee chimed in with amusement, "Hey: is your cat wearing a purple t-shirt?"

What I'm telling you here is that purple t-shirt wearing cats are the enemy to effective Zoom meeting productivity.

Also, there is a real blurring of the lines between different parts of your life. The same room you are zooming out of is where you now talk to your boss, say hi to your friends and toast a glass of wine, chat with your children's teacher about their math, and have a date with someone new or date night with your spouse.

Finally, you're also conscious of the environment that your audience is in: you are peering into their lives, their home office set-up, and the act looking into each of their lives and seeing their world as disrupted and disjointed as ours is a reminder that all of us are going through this upside-down funhouse mirror experience of the pandemic, where there isn't any boundary between home and work.

Reduced Mobility

Your camera has a field of view. When you are on a Zoom, you are constrained to stay seated within that field of view. This can make you feel trapped in a way, and limited on what you can do. As well, it's fatiguing to be sitting all day. If you've ever been on a twelve-hour flight, you know what I'm talking about. You crave standing up, stretching and walking around. Staying in a frozen, sedentary position is energy depleting. Additionally, it can prove to be harmful overall for your posture – desks that allow you to stand at your work station have become more prominent in the last few years for this very reason. Finally, when you're on Zoom, you have to stay close to the keyboard in case you need to type an answer or hit the unmute button, further freezing you in position.

Solutions to Zoom Fatigue

Turn Off Your Camera

The obvious solution to feeling self-conscious is removing yourself from view. This is something that would benefit from being encouraged by the speaker if it makes sense – for example, if the speaker is sharing their screen and presenting a slide deck. No need for the cameras to be on. It gives you the comfort that you can stretch, stand up, get up from your chair and walk back – all of which will set you at greater ease. However, if the meeting is collaborative and people are exchanging ideas, it would be unnerving for the speaker to be staring into space. There are times when it makes sense to have everyone's camera on. But if you don't need to, then encourage everyone to take a break from it and treat the meeting exactly as you would a teleconference in days gone by.

Have Your Own Space (If Possible)

My wife, being an HR Director, has had to contend with this in a big way. At the beginning of the pandemic, we made the dining table our "schoolroom" for our son and he was situated there throughout the day, logging into Google Classroom, getting his work done, and doing Google Hangouts with the class. I was beside him on and off through the day assisting him with his work and keeping him on track.

I have a personal office in our home; a room above the garage, with its own little staircase and door. It was one of the reasons we bought the house, since I've been self-employed for almost twenty years and worked out of my home. So when the pandemic hit, it was no problem for me to hunker down, close the door and deliver presentations without distraction.

My wife was an entirely different story. Her role demanded privacy because of the nature of the conversations she had, but also because at her level she needed to generate a lot of strategy and lead some high-level initiatives. She needed her own space. Shortly into the pandemic, an Ikea desk was purchased, a corner of the master bedroom reorganized, and this became my wife's new permanent home-office space. (In addition, she loves to paint and make creations on her Cricut, and this space doubles as her personal art centre.)

Why do you NEED to do a video Call?

Because it's so easy to jump on a Zoom call, people might start deferring to it automatically. But you don't need to do a Zoom in every circumstance. The phone has worked great for generations, helping people maintain relationships and build business empires. One of the smartest things we can do right now is say "no" to a Zoom when a phone call would do. Or, at the very least, gently suggest that you switch formats and see if the other person is amenable to doing so. It gives you a bit of variety in the way you communicate. It lets us get up and walk around, which gets the heart pumping and creates some energy. It allows you to multitask if that's appropriate; you can take a call and be making lunch on the stove at the same time, or throwing on a load of laundry. It lets you pace while you discuss ideas. Because you aren't physically constrained by your chair, you might feel more inspired creatively. And since we're all getting tired of staring at a camera, it lets your eyes have a rest.

Give Your Eyes a Break

When someone spends the day staring at a screen, their eyes become fatigued from the constant stare, and they become irritated as we hold our eyes open longer. The solution to this is the 20-20-20 method, which suggests that every 20 minutes you should look away from your screen and focus instead on something that is 20 feet away, for 20 seconds.[lxxxiii] On top of that, just give your eyes a rest and close them completely for 20 seconds! A final tip: try getting in the habit that every time you click on a link, you blink. It's a little behavioural reminder to give your eyes a break.

Making Sure Everyone is Speaking Up

Another problem that participants in Zoom meetings face is that it can be harder to get a word in edgewise. In a live meeting, you can use body language to interject. In a virtual meeting, a digital raised hand can more easily be missed or even go ignored by the host. This can leave employees feeling disengaged rather than being active, valued participants in the meeting. The solution is to for the meeting host to ensure that everyone gets a chance to be heard. In his book *Smarter Faster Better*, author Charles Duhigg shares this exact strategy as gleaned by an internal study at Google. They found that managers that promoted psychological safety seemed to have higher-performing and more cohesive teams. The trick for meetings? Make sure everyone in the team had a moment to share their thoughts. Smart managers would keep a list of all meeting participants and put a tick next to each name as the meeting progressed.[lxxxiv] If someone hadn't spoken up, the smart manager would make a point to engage them at some point to ask their thoughts on what was being discussed. They wouldn't adjourn the meeting until everyone had spoken. If that becomes cumbersome, build more time into the meeting for interactions, check earlier in the meeting that everyone has spoken up, or have a smaller meeting with Zoom fewer people. There are going to be examples where this isn't practical: you may have one thousand people in your department on the Zoom. The principle is still good: where reasonable, make sure people are involved and speaking up.

Stand Up and Stretch

The most repetitive strain injury prior to the pandemic wasn't carpal tunnel – it was sitting. Ask any chiropractor if sitting in a chair all day is good for your spine, and you will receive a lengthy dissertation on the virtues of a standing desk. If you aren't ready, willing or able to make that purchase, just make a point of standing throughout your day. Since we get swept up in the business of our day and often neglect self-care, try making it a part of your meeting kick-offs, or have a half-time 30-second stretch, and just watch people perk right up.

In conclusion, the prevalence and ease-of-use of web conferencing technology has allowed the incalculable benefit of allowing us to stay connected with clients, colleagues and loved ones while maintaining safe habits through social distancing. But too much of anything can become overwhelming and overshadow the perceived benefit. By incorporating these strategies outlined here, you can reduce your virtual fatigue and take away one more of the stressors the pandemic has added to our day.

CHAPTER 6:
YOUR STRESS MOSQUITOS

"You can't calm the storm – so stop trying. What you can do is calm yourself. The storm will pass." – Timber Hawkeye

Stress levels have skyrocketed around the globe during COVID-19. There are legitimate and specific stressors that are uniquely caused by the pandemic, such as fear of contracting the virus, fear for our family's health and safety, the economic downturn, isolation and missing out on socializing, the pressures of working from home, the pressures of helping kids with distance learning – the list can feel endless.

Because of the stress the pandemic is causing, we wake up a little more stressed than we normally. Perhaps pre-COVID you started each day at a 3/10 stressed. Now, maybe you start each day at a 6/10 stressed. What that means is you're already a little on edge, a little more run down, and the little stressors that wouldn't have normally set you off are more likely to seem magnified in your mind.

As well, the pandemic has exacerbated the stress experience for people who were already suffering from mental health issues. They are less likely to go get help because they may not want to go outside to the counselor or medical clinic. Counselors are less available, with the amount of mental health issues climbing sharply this year, filling up their schedules. And they themselves are feeling the strain because of the increased workload, and in some circumstances they are getting burned out themselves.

Managing stress during COVID has its own particular challenge because some of the techniques you would use to bring comfort are no longer available. Not only do you lose the renewing benefit of the fun activity, you also mourn its absence – which creates more stress.

It's valuable at this point to remind ourselves is that stress has always been part of the human experience, and will continue long after we've defeated COVID-19. The pandemic has absolutely created additional stress, but what about the stressors we faced before? We faced day-to-day stressors like work deadlines, disagreements with family, angry clients, a flooded basement, the Wi-Fi going down, the kids leaving a mess in the sink, or someone leaving the cap off of the toothpaste. We also faced major stressors before COVID-19, such as family members falling ill or passing away, divorce, job loss, or natural disasters.

It might be helpful to separate these categories in our minds, differentiating "COVID-19 related" stress from the usual "day-to-day" stress. With so many *big* problems facing us, we still need some strategies to handle the *little* things.

All of those little stressors still exist through the pandemic, but we feel it more intensely right now. It's similar to being bumped when you have a sunburn: although the other person didn't touch you that hard, the pain is much more intense because of how sensitive your injured skin is. The slightest touch radiates pain.

What this chapter offers is a bit of a "pressure valve" for managing the daily stressors that were already troubling before COVID-19, and now might feel overwhelming. What we're talking about is the nitty-gritty daily triggers that can sour your mood and tick you off. Not the world-ending stuff; just the little things. Daily stress is like a mosquito in a camping tent at night. It won't kill you, but it sure will ruin your peace. The little mosquito wrecks our sleep, leaving us less effective at facing the big problems we might face the next day – and we have far too many real problems right now to be getting twisted up in knots over comparatively little things. We still need a way to swat the annoying little mosquitos that are bugging us – the flat tires and the dirty dishes. And that is what this final chapter is all about.

What Is Stress?

"Worry is like a rocking chair: it gives you something to do but never gets you anywhere." – Erma Bombeck

Stress is not the event that happens in front of us, or the person who exhibits behaviour in our presence that we find "irritating"… stress is our *reaction* to those things. Stress is our emotional and physiological response to any perceived threat, whether real or imagined. The most important word in that definition is the word *perceived*, because the event doesn't even need to be real in order for you to experience stress. It could be a scary nightmare, an overwhelming phobia or a drug-induced hallucination. Your body will respond as if you are actually in physical danger. This response is called the "fight-or-flight" response.

The fight-or-flight response (otherwise known as the stress response) is our rapid physiological response to a mortal threat, for example at the hands of a predator. To quickly summarize, this response gives you an immediate surge of energy that allows you either to run for your life away from the predator (flight) or if you cannot run fast enough, to turn and defend yourself even if it is a fight to the death (fight).

Scientists also show that there is a third option, "freeze", where an animal will become paralyzed when encountering a predator in an instinctual effort to remain unseen. This can be seen in the well-intended but ill-advised tendency of animals to freeze on the highway when caught in the headlights of automobiles. For the simplicity of our discussion we will choose to focus on fight and flight.

Let's suppose you are in a situation where you perceive a mortal threat: you are camping in the woods and you run into a bear. This is generally regarded as a threatening situation to life and limb! Here is what happens:

Stage 1: The Event Occurs. Whatever the threatening event is, whether it is running into a bear in the woods, almost colliding with a van on the highway, having a family member fall ill – or having to deliver a speech in front of a crowd.

Stage 2: Your Evaluation. This is where you decided whether or not the event is worth getting stressed out over. You soak in all of the data from the situation through your five senses: visual (sight), auditory (sound), kinesthetic (touch), olfactory (smell) and gustatory (taste/digestion). You consider all of the millions of bits of data within a split second to decide whether or not this situation is dangerous. If you decide it is, you are going to get stressed. However, if you don't think it is worth getting stressed over, you just simply aren't going to get stressed. Your evaluation literally has the power to make-or-break your stress response on the spot. If you are walking down the highway and you are about to be run down by a truck, but you don't hear or see it coming, you aren't going to get stressed, even though you are in mortal danger. However, if you decide you ARE in danger, you go to the next stage…

Stage 3: Chemical Response. Once you've decided you're in danger, your hypothalamus recruits the sympathetic nervous system. A signal is sent to your adrenaline glands to begin producing adrenaline, cortisol & cortisone[lxxxv]. These in turn create a cascade of physiological reactions

Stage 4: Physiological Reaction. In response to the chemicals flooding your body, your body gears up so that you can either run for your life, or fight to the death. Some of the reactions commonly associated with this fight-or-flight response include:

- Increased heart rate and blood pressure to make blood delivery more efficient
- Diversion of blood from less essential systems (like digestion) to most life-saving essential systems
- Shortness of breath from rapid, shallow breathing
- Heightened sense of sight and hearing
- Increased energy by releasing glucose stores
- Surge of endorphins to block pain signals from any injury sustained in the fight
- The release of cortisol also limits or stops activity in other less-essential systems like the immune system or the reproductive system
- Your liver begins releasing additional energy stores (such as fat and cholesterol)

This is a *really* good reaction, if you are actually in danger. If a bear is chasing you, it's a really good response to be able to run faster than you've ever run, to be able to cut off the pain signal to your brain and ignore small injuries, to have superhuman strength to be able to defend yourself.

You've probably heard anecdotal stories of people trapped in life-and-death circumstances who were possessed with super human strength; people who have lifted cars off of family members or ripped a car door off of its hinges to save someone.[lxxxvi] A combination of adrenaline, glucose stores and endorphins combine to make the person seem invincible.

This stress response is extremely taxing on your nervous system, and once the danger has abated, your body would feel exhaustion. Your body can handle it though, since you probably aren't often in mortal danger. Consider how often you face a legitimate physical threat – perhaps once every ten years. But how often might you feel stressed? Maybe once every ten minutes! The point being, we are wildly overreacting and overusing a helpful biological defense to the point that it becomes unhelpful – specifically in the many situations where we would benefit far more by keeping our cool and remaining calm.

Most Fears Are Learned

"There is great beauty in going through life without anxiety or fear. Half our fears are baseless, and the other half discreditable." – John Christian Boyee

Most of the time when we get stressed, we are not in physical danger. The danger we fear is almost always a figment of our imagination. Babies are born with only two natural fears: the fear of loud noises, and the fear of falling. Thus, anything else that you fear is a *learned* fear. This doesn't de-legitimize your stress if a loved one is ill, particularly during this pandemic. But most of the stressors we face in daily life don't involve our family members being in the ICU. Many of our stressors are overreactions to the situation we face.

Let me give you a very common example: public speaking. The technical term for this fear is glossophobia. I've heard a statistic which states that speaking in front of an audience is the #1 fear for most people. Isn't that amazing! (I guess I'm strange in that I get excited by the size of the audience; give me 5000 people for a few hours and I'm in Heaven! But I clearly recognize that this would be terrifying for most people.)

Consider what happens for a person mentally, physically and emotionally when they start to get scared. What sort of words are they saying to themselves? Are they saying *"Wow! I'm an incredible speaker! These people look so happy to see me!"*, or do you think they might be saying something else? Without question, they are saying things like *"I'm going to screw up, I'm going to forget what I was supposed to say, my PowerPoint will crash, I'll make a fool of myself, everyone is staring at me, I feel so embarrassed, and this is going to be terrible!"*

When a person starts saying these things to themselves, what do you suppose starts to happen to their heart rate? It increases. What about their rate of breath? Are they breathing slow, relaxed, deep breaths? No; their breathing is rapid and shallow. In fact, they might even be holding their breath. What about their hands; are they calm and steady? No; their hands are shaking along with their knees, because all of the adrenaline coursing through their body is making them shake. What about their digestive tract? Is their tummy nice and relaxed? No, it feels like their stomach is doing somersaults. The nickname for this queasy feeling is "butterflies in your stomach". This feeling is occurring because blood is being diverted away from their digestive tract. These reactions, along with a host of others, are all the same reactions that occur in times of extreme stress when you believe you are in mortal danger. However, when you are speaking, you aren't in mortal danger. *(Unless you're really bad!)* However, you might believe that you are in social danger, fearing that you will be ostracized, laughed at, singled out, made fun of, etc.

This raises a critical point as to why people are so stressed: the human mind does not distinguish between something that is actually happening versus something that is vividly imagined. That's how you can have a scary, violent nightmare and wake up with the sheets soaked with sweat and your heart is racing. As far as your brain is concerned, the scary images in your imagination may as well be real, since they *seemed* real enough. Once the "launch sequence" is initiated in your fight-or-flight response, it is very difficult to interrupt.

It's Actually Good to Have Some Stress

"It is not in the still calm of life, or the repose of a pacific station, that great characters are formed.... Great necessities call out great virtues." – Abigail Adams

Contrary to popular belief, it's actually a good idea to have a *little* bit of stress in life. The opposite of stress is boredom. Without any pressures, any deadlines, anything challenging us to perform, we will just slack off and lay around the poolside, sipping margaritas and playing yet another round of golf before we get our afternoon massage. (You might be thinking "that doesn't sound so bad!")

Of course, it *sounds* great! In fact, it's great for about a week; maximum two weeks. But after that short time, you start getting restless. You may have heard of this experience; it's called "cabin fever". People are *not* meant to be terminally lazy and directionless. We are goal-achieving animals and we don't do well to have eons of unstructured time. (This is one of the reasons why retirement can be such a challenge for people who were highly productive on the job, and then don't have a full schedule of activities planned for their newfound time off.) It can start to feel very unpleasant just sitting around doing nothing.

When we have just the right amount of stress, we are motivated to push ourselves beyond our normal limits and achieve extraordinary results. I'm sure we've all had days where the stakes were high, the chips were down and somehow we miraculously managed to accomplish what seemed almost impossible at the time. And isn't it true that when we pull off a seemingly miraculous accomplishment, we feel absolutely incredible! That sort of pride in beating the odds can make you feel invincible, and you get to spend the rest of the day walking around like you are ten feet tall. This is the moment where stress in an incalculable asset: with just enough pressure, your true genius is revealed.

Tom Kiatipis, Canadian bodybuilding champion and founder of the League of Elite fitness program, says, "Through COVID-19, the lockdowns, the uncertainty, the madness; it all has an effect on you. That's for certain. What are you going to do about it? How can you turn things around for you and your family? Its times like this that courage under fire will expose you or bring to light the strength you have inside of you. Which do you choose?"

Stress becomes a problem when we tip past the point of stress being a benefit, and instead of looking at a problem as a challenge to be overcome we view it as an insurmountable obstacle that will crush us. Whether real or imagined, if you don't think you can handle the problem you face, if you think that it is too big, coming at you too fast, or that you don't have the skills and experience to pull off a victory, you're going to get stressed.

What Are The Consequences?

"You don't get ulcers from what you eat. You get them from what's eating you." – Vicki Baum

If you don't learn to manage your stress, do you believe that eventually your health will suffer? Absolutely! In fact, the pioneering father of stress research, Montreal doctor Hans Selye, says that *"Mental tensions, frustrations, insecurity, aimlessness are among the most damaging stressors, and psychosomatic studies have shown how often they cause migraine headache, peptic ulcers, heart attacks, hypertension, mental disease, suicide, or just hopeless unhappiness."* Here are some of the potential consequences of unmanaged stress, from the mundane to the life-threatening:

- Fatigue
- Irritability
- Muscle tension, particularly in our neck, shoulders and back
- Lack of concentration
- Forgetfulness
- Gastro-intestinal challenges including stomach upset, diarrhea, and ulcers
- Compromised immune system
- Cardiovascular challenges, including increased blood pressure or hypertension
- Heart attack

- Stroke

With all of the possible negative consequences, it is vital that we take positive action to mitigate the stressors we face in our daily lives and enjoy a more relaxed, enjoyable day!

What Are Your Triggers?

"Getting angry is actually punishing yourself for the mistakes of others." - Unknown

Since people can respond differently to the same situation, it's valuable to identify the things that you know will cause you to feel frustrated. I've provided a checklist below of behaviours or situations that might "stress you out". Knowing your triggers allows you to develop coping strategies in advance; it also allows you to communicate to the people around you what your sensitivities are so that they can minimize any innocent missteps.

Pandemic-specific situations:

- Ourselves or a loved one contracting COVID-19
- Losing a loved one to the virus
- Financial pressure due to loss of work
- Isolation from other people

- Missing out on special events, holiday gatherings, celebrations, graduations, dances, weddings, funerals, attending live church, attending concerts and movies, missing seeing extended friends and family outside your "bubble"
- Essential workers facing increased risk of exposure to COVID-19
- For those working from home, the impact on work/life balance
- The stress of needing to stay hyper vigilant with mask-wearing, hand washing and social distancing
- Worrying about the safety and wellbeing of our loved ones
- OTHER: _____

Daily life Situations:

- When ourselves or a loved one faces a health challenge
- Facing any financial pressure
- Facing increased work load or job challenges
- arranging a wedding ceremony
- sleepless nights with a new baby
- Anytime we are fighting physical discomfort, illness, fatigue, migraine headaches, stomach upset, etc.
- caught in traffic
- stuck in a lineup at the grocery store
- the alarm clock doesn't go off
- buying a new home and moving in
- technology problems: the PowerPoint won't work, etc., our computer hard drive crashes, our spam folder accidentally catches and deletes an important email

- OTHER: _____

Behaviours. When other people:

- are upset with you, but won't admit to it when asked
- use passive/aggressive behaviour to sabotage you instead of dealing with a problem directly
- use insulting or hurtful remarks
- invade your personal space
- make threatening gestures
- speak loudly on their cell phone
- cut you off in the middle of speaking
- finish your sentences for you
- use profanity
- raise their voice
- over-commit and under-deliver
- act like a doormat and accept bad behaviour
- can't make a decision
- lie
- cheat
- betray your trust
- break your confidence and share your secrets with others
- blame you for their mistakes
- take credit for your accomplishments
- always hog all of the attention
- are totally irresponsible
- are disorganized and lose everything
- are chronically late for meetings and appointments
- are thoughtless and devoid of empathy

- are selfish or greedy
- are obnoxiously competitive
- are compulsive perfectionists
- don't return phone calls or emails
- won't answer questions directly
- won't keep their promises
- speed while driving
- don't signal when changing lanes
- cut you off while changing lanes
- OTHER: _____

We cause ourselves stress by:

- procrastination
- disorganization
- losing important documents
- can't find our car keys
- cell phone isn't charged
- not saving for "rainy day" emergencies
- not planning meals ahead of time so we eat junk food, or we eat nothing at all
- haven't confirmed hotel reservations
- running out of gasoline, not checking our tires, or not changing our oil
- not taking care of our health through poor diet, lack of exercise, not getting a check-up with our doctor
- ignoring our most valuable relationships
- snapping in frustration at the people we love
- OTHER: _____

STRATEGIES FOR REDUCING STRESS

Now that we've discussed the four stages of the fight-or-flight response and looked at some common triggers for stress, we have use that understanding to design some powerful strategies to mitigate our stress. Let's go down the list, from stage 1 to stage 4, and create strategies to literally stop our stress in its tracks!

Stage 1: Stop the Event from Happening

"Worrying about things you cannot control is folly. Focus only on those few things you have any control over, and your life becomes much simpler." – Jeffrey Fry

It just makes sense that if you know what triggers your stress, you can more effectively avoid the trigger, and then you will avoid feeling stressed. For example, if traffic jams tend to frustrate you, then if you watch your GPS, listen to the news or look at the internet highway traffic cameras you can pinpoint where the accident is and drive around it. The result: you avoid the trigger of your stress, so you avoid the stress itself!

As we've discussed, there are many things in life you can't control, and many that you can. Suppose for example that the thing that is causing you stress is being late getting to work. Your boss has warned you that being late one more time will result in disciplinary actions.

Now, there are many possible strategies to managing the stress of being late. You could do yoga, or deep breathing, or watch a funny sitcom, or imagine a "happy place", or eat some chocolate.

But what do you suppose might be a more effective way of managing the stress of being late?

You got it: *don't be late.* Use every strategy you can imagine to get your little buns out the door on time: wake up earlier, have two alarms, move the alarm clock so it's across the room and you have to get up, have your morning tasks done the night before, etc. This is a triggering event you can control – so control it.

Start applying this to every stress trigger. Start asking yourself "Is there any way that I can control this event from happening?" If it is possible to prevent it from happening, stop it quickly if it has happened or minimize its impact, then you will manage the stress quite well.

Consider the stress of having a fire potentially break out on your stove. The three steps to managing this from creating stress are Prevent, Stop and Minimize.

Prevent: Don't put anything flammable near the stove, and don't leave the stove unattended while on. This will prevent a fire.

Stop: If a fire starts, you could have planned ahead and had a fire extinguisher next to the stove to stop the fire from spreading and getting any worse if it does start.

Minimize: If you can't stop the fire, you can minimize the total damage inflicted (and total stress created!) by ensuring your family's safety by installing smoke alarms in the house with new batteries, practice fire drills and develop escape plans for your family including rope ladders out of upstairs windows. You can also have enough fire insurance to pay for any damage.

Think about how you might apply this to a situation that consistently frustrates you. What you want to do is look for patterns; if something happens once a week, and has happened every week for the last couple of months, there is a good chance it is going to happen again this week and you're going to get frustrated.

For example, suppose your manager comes to you Friday at 4:59 each week and says "I'm so sorry, I just need you to finish this up before you leave," and they hand you an hour of paperwork to be completed. That might be frustrating! But if they do it all the time, you can expect it and try to find a solution. Perhaps you could set an email reminder to yourself for 4:00 to go to their desk and ask them if they have any work that needs to be completed by 5:00, since you'll be leaving at that time to pick up your kids promptly from day care. There's a good chance they've had the work sitting on their desk all day and they've simply forgotten to pass it onto you! One simple action on your part and the stressful situation is averted.

When our son was just a little guy, he would constantly be losing his socks. At the time, the morning routine around our house was controlled chaos as we were all night owls. So each morning, we would race around the house getting him ready for pre-school and elementary school, and we would always – always – struggle to find matching socks. So, one day I got fed up with this problem, noting that I could predict it was going to continue ceaselessly until something changed. I marched into Walmart, went to the shelf with little boy socks, and swept the entire shelf into my basket. Eighty-six pairs of matching grey socks found a new home that evening in our son's drawer. After that, we never again searched for matching socks. As he outgrew them or lost them, I would repeat the same process and replenish his supply.

You probably have multiple little frustrations that you face through your day. Start addressing them one by one. If it seems easier, begin with the easiest, simplest problems and rid yourself of those. It's more stress-relieving to rid yourself of big problems, but you'll more quickly feel motivated and get momentum by tackling the little ones; they just feel more controllable. Watch as your day starts to get easier as you remove the little irritants, freeing you up to tackle the legitimately challenging problems.

Once you've done everything you can to address every problem you can control, you move onto using the next strategy:

Stage #2: Control Your Perspective

"You can't always have a good day. But you can always face a bad day with a good attitude." - Unknown

If you can't stop or control the situation that causes you stress (Stage #1), your next option is to control your evaluation (Stage #2). Whatever your perspective, if you think something is worth getting stressed out over it, you're going to get stressed. The simple solution at this point is to remember that your perspective or "attitude" has massive control over your stress response. Remember that a person can be paralyzed with fear because of an intense phobia like claustrophobia in an elevator, whereas other people remain totally calm. Your positive perspective can either throw proverbial water on the fire of your stress, or your negative perspective can throw gasoline on the fire. If you choose to perceive something as a threat, your body will respond as if it actually were. We've already discussed changing your story in the earlier chapter on resilience, so take action and implement all of the tools that I've shared the next time you face a situation that challenges your patience. These are the tools that I personally use!

Consider a common example many people have faced. Imagine it's Tuesday morning and your boss emails you to say, "I'd like to talk with you at 4:30 today… here's the Zoom link for you to join me then."

Now, what do you suppose the average employee thinks is going to happen to them at 4:30?

That's right – they probably think they are getting fired. Or, certainly reprimanded/ yelled at/ in trouble/ chastised.

Going back to our earlier story of three people in the elevator, let me remind you of this question: it is the boss's words that cause the employee fear? Or, is it the employee's story that they are telling themselves that is causing them fear? You guessed it: the employee's story is causing them fear. So, what we have to do is change our perspective by changing our story.

Ask yourself, "Other than getting in trouble, what could be a positive possible alternative reason for the meeting? What could be an example that is good?"

Then, start to brainstorm your answers. You can probably come up with a dozen possible alternatives that are positive. The boss wants to:

- ask me a question
- ask my advice and expertise on solving a problem
- let me know they are going on vacation
- take over a meeting next week for them
- enroll in a leadership mentoring program
- pay me a compliment
- give me a promotion and a raise!

By deliberating choosing to consider positive alternatives, you shift your mind from worrying to consider that something good might happen. The result? You probably calm down and have a productive and stress-free afternoon.

Stage #3: Manage Your Chemical Intake

"Chocolate comes from cocoa, which is a tree. That makes it a plant. Chocolate is therefore salad." - Unknown

If you can't stop the event from happening, and if you can't keep a positive attitude, your body sends a signal to your adrenal gland and you go into the third stage: your chemical response. While it is unlikely that you will have conscious control over the production of these chemicals, we must also recognize that any chemicals we introduce in our body can soothe or exacerbate our stress response. (The strategies that I'm sharing here are all related to managing the chemicals in our body, although admittedly I'm going to be describing chemicals other that adrenaline and cortisol. Just for simplicity I've decided to group all of these concepts together and describe them in this section.)

Some people then turn to chemicals to manage their stress levels. This is rarely a good idea, most particularly if you are the one administering the chemicals. One of the most common ways of altering you moods is by drinking alcohol. I don't ever suggest drinking to manage anxiety or depression. (For the record, I don't like the bitter taste of beer and wine and never drink it. I also don't like the dizzy experience of intoxication, so I just don't do it.) There is nothing wrong with having a glass of wine or a bottle of beer, but please use moderation with alcohol. I also don't agree with using illegal drugs. It's obvious, though, that many people use drugs and alcohol to lift their spirits or drown their sorrows. It was telling here in Ontario that since the first lockdown, the LCBO and the Beer Store have always been considered an essential service and remained open for business. In fact, the Canadian Centre on Substance Use and Addiction reports that 18% of Canadians, or roughly one in five, have increased their alcohol consumption during COVID-19.[lxxxvii]

In cases like depression or overwhelming anxiety, I would recommend that you consult a psychiatrist, or at the very least your family doctor. If a psychiatrist prescribes anti-depressant medication, by all means follow the prescription. But please don't alter the prescription and think "I know the doctor said only take one pill a day, but today is Monday and I've had a really bad time at work... I'm going to take 5 pills!" That is a profoundly *bad idea*. Always follow the directions of a psychiatrist in these cases.

There is one final way of ingesting chemicals to manage your mood. It is very popular, much less insidious, and completely legal. It is called eating "comfort food". You've probably heard this term. The reason for the name is that the food tends to comfort people. Food never cheats on you, never lets you down, it's always there at 2am when you're feeling down, and it won't talk about you behind your back. It's like a trusted and loyal friend for many people. The most popular form of comfort food seems to be chocolate! My own personal experience suggests that women tend to eat chocolate to lift their spirits more than men do. Do you know why? Because it works!

When you ingest chocolate, it causes a release of a neurotransmitter called endorphins. Endorphins have the same chemical structure as morphine, yet they are 100 times more powerful. They block the pain signal from reaching the brain during times of high stress, so that if you are injured in a fight you literally will not feel it until after the fight is done. But a massive dose of endorphins causes you to feel euphoric... you just simply feel happy! Chocolate can help with this, which is one reason for its popularity (along with the fact it tastes great). But again, all things in moderation: don't go eating slabs of chocolate when you're depressed. Overeating obviously leads to obesity and a host of related health challenges.

In conclusion, there is rarely a good chemical-related stress management strategy that I'm going to recommend (unless prescribed by a psychiatrist). So if you don't drink the problem away, what's left to manage your stress?

Stage #4: Change Your Physiology

"For fast-acting relief try slowing down." – Lily Tomlin

And finally, if you can't stop the situation (Stage #1), you can't look at it positively (Stage #2), you wisely choose not to drink the problem away (Stage #3), you are now in full-fledged fight-or-flight response. Your heart rate has dramatically accelerated, your breathing is rapid and shallow, your digestive system is shutting down and adrenaline is coursing through your body. You are sitting at your desk, driving your car, or sitting at your kitchen table, and you are stressed out. So, now what? Because the stress reaction is a PHYSICAL REACTION in your body, it demands a physiological intervention in order to calm yourself down at this point. So what's the best way to calm down your body? The top three interventions I recommend at this stage are Exercise, Laughter and Deep Breathing.

Deep Breathing. This is the fastest, easiest, most appropriate tool in the most number of situations. The reason it works is because when we are in fight-or-flight mode, we start breathing rapid, shallow breaths. This gives a quick influx of oxygen. But then we hold our breath, particularly when we are exerting ourselves by sprinting or exerting our muscles in a fight. Think of any time you are exercising at the gym and lifting heavy weights, or you pick up something really heavy, or you sprint up a flight of stairs. The chances are that once you stop at the top of the stairs, you realize that you were holding your breath the entire time! Try it and you'll see what I'm talking about. Why do we do this? Because in fight-or-flight mode, our brain is making very quick decisions about where to spend energy and where to save it. All of us can hold our breath for a short period of time, because we are very inefficient with processing oxygen. When we breathe in air, it is 24% oxygen, and when we exhale, what we exhale still contains 16% oxygen. This is how we are able to do CPR and deliver some oxygen to our patient by blowing into their mouth. Since the average person can hold their breath for about 30 seconds, your brain decides during intense situations that for the next 30 seconds, you are simply going to skip breathing! The reason that deep breathing works is that you are taking conscious control over your body's stress reaction. Unless you are a Tibetan monk, you likely don't have conscious control over your heart rate or your adrenal glands, but everyone can choose to breathe more slowly. When you breathe slow, deep breaths in, pause, and slowly exhale, you put the brakes on your whole sympathetic nervous system and you calm yourself right down. The great thing is that you can use this strategy in almost every situation: while you are driving, at home or at your desk at work.

Exercise. Please remember that during the fight-or-flight response, your body wants to either run, or fight. Your heart is pounding, your hands are shaking with adrenaline… your body is primed for action. So what can you do to relax? You go and exercise! Exercise is a fantastic way of burning off the stress response and returning you to homeostasis (the body's normal state of stress-free calm). So go and exercise! Just remember to do intense exercise in order to mimic the intensity of running or fighting; light or moderate exercise at this stage may not be sufficient.

Laughter. A friend shared with me, "Due to the lockdown, I'll only be telling inside jokes." Enjoy a laugh today! This is my #1 favorite stress-managing technique. For the same reason as chocolate, laughter is an excellent stress-reliever because it causes a surge of endorphins. Most people have figured out that laughter makes them feel good, even if they don't understand the chemistry behind it. They just know that if they go home and watch their favorite sit-com like *The Office* or *The Big Bang Theory* they'll feel better. So, since you now understand this, why don't your purposely add more humour to your day. Read the comics, watch funny videos (just not when you're supposed to be working!), or watch funny movies. One of my favorite things to do is listening to comedy audios while I drive my car in traffic. I already know that I'm going to get stuck in traffic occasionally; why wouldn't I try to find a way to enjoy it more? You end up laughing all the way to work and all the way back home, and you get to your destination in a great mood!

All of these strategies are common sense, and you probably knew about and agreed with most all of them. The issue isn't whether you know a good way to reduce stress; it's whether you can remember to use the strategy when you're stressed. That's when it's hard to remember! So, however you need to do it, you've got to figure out a way of reminding yourself to follow through on these strategies. Sometimes I will write a note to myself on the back of my business card and keep it in my pocket; every time I need it, it's right there to remind me. Maybe you put a Post-it note on your computer monitor. Whatever you do, pick a few key strategies and implement them when the pressure is on. If you do so, you're going to find that problems don't seem as big as they used to, your day gets easier, you start having more fun and life is simply more enjoyable on a daily basis!

50 Tips to Reduce Stress

What follows is a list of stress-reduction tips and tricks that I've amassed over the years. As you scan down the list, put a checkmark next to the tips that you think might be helpful and enjoyable for you!

- Count to ten
- Smile more often
- Eat nutritious food that energizes you
- Listen to your favorite music
- Play games with friends
- Share a joke with a friend
- Dress in a way that makes you feel good
- Wake up at the same time each day to avoid morning fatigue
- Talk to a trusted friend
- Stop and smell the roses
- Plan ahead
- If possible, avoid situations that cause you stress
- Ask "What's positive about this?"
- Read a good book
- Watch your favorite TV program
- Get some fresh air
- Change your focus
- Know your limits
- Play some games
- Enjoy your favorite hobby

- Avoid coffee, drink juice and water instead
- Don't blame yourself
- Ask for help
- Realize that "This too shall pass"
- Leave your work at the office
- Partake in a massage
- Enjoy a catnap
- Soak in a warm bubble bath
- Always, ALWAYS, take a lunch break
- Get some sleep
- Find the silver lining
- Plan your time
- Prioritize
- Get organized
- Be on time to meetings
- If you are worried, just prepare more
- When you're feeling down, volunteer and help someone else
- Don't avoid a problem and let it grow
- Clear your conscience
- Act with integrity
- Speak positively of others
- Notice what you do right and feel proud of yourself
- Dale Carnegie says "Don't condemn, complain or criticize"
- Admit your mistakes
- Deep breathing
- Intense Exercise
- Stretch
- Take a yoga or Pilates class

- Put on your favorite music, get up and dance!
- Squeeze a stress ball

In conclusion, stress is always going to be part of our lives. By using these techniques, we can reduce the number of things that upset us, we can reduce our reaction to them, and have a practiced set of tools at the ready that we can employ to have a happier, more relaxed, and fulfilling day.

Conclusion

We've come to the end of the book, but hopefully not to the end of our time together. This book is meant to serve as a guide, and it's my hope that you find it helpful to return to these pages when the need arises.

It's been my experience that whenever I am presented with a new concept or strategy, the very best way that I can ensure it takes root in my life is to take action on that new knowledge as quickly as possible. I like to ask myself, "How can I apply this today?" I find it helpful when I reach the end of a book to actually return to the beginning, and briefly review the key highlights or (if you read with a pen in your hand like I do) the underlined passages and notes I've left for myself in the margins. I encourage you to take a moment and flip back through the book to land on the ideas that resonated most with you.

A final powerful strategy I use is I like to teach what I've learned to someone else. I find that by talking it out over coffee, or over Zoom, or even by writing an article or an email to my team, it highlights what I've learned and where I need to refresh my memory. When I teach information, I find I start to take ownership of what I've learned. If you've found these ideas helpful, I'd love to hear from you, and hear about how you are doing through this challenging time. You can reach me at cj@cjcalvert.com. If you are a leader in an organization and you feel these ideas would benefit your staff, I would be pleased to discuss how I might best serve you and your team. Wishing you health, happiness and prosperity,

CJ Calvert

ADDITIONAL RESOURCES

COVID-19 INFORMATION RESOURCES

COVID-19 Information for Canadians
https://www.canada.ca/en/public-health/services/diseases/coronavirus-disease-covid-19.html

WHO - World Health Organization
who.int

CDC – Centres for Disease Control and Infection
cdc.gov

MENTAL HEALTH RESOURCES

Bell Let's Talk & Kid's Help Phone
letstalk.bell.ca
kidshelpphone.ca

CAMH: The Centre for Addiction and Mental Health
camh.ca

Canadian Mental Health Association
Cmha.ca

Acknowledgements

Like all books, a debt of gratitude is owed to the beautiful people who have been part of this adventure.

Thank you to my dearest Shannon and beloved Braydon for your patience, love, and grace. Shannon, your brilliance and depth astound me every day – I won the lottery with you. Braydon, you are the most wonderful young man I have the privilege to know; anyone would be lucky to call you a friend. You are kind, witty, creative and resilient. You are such a fine young man; one day, you'll make an amazing husband and father.

To all my friends and family who have supported and encouraged me along this journey: Jhan & Bill, Jim & Kit, Craig & Emma, Linda, Tom & the League of Elite, Steve & Lisa Stokl, Bill Tibbo, Joanna Burke, Thanh, and my colleagues at Life Works/Morneau Shepell: Sadek, Elena, Jacenta, and the gang – thank you for your positive impact on my work and life.

About the Author

CJ Calvert is a professional speaker and author, delivering training to corporate audiences across North America. For the last two decades CJ has spoken on a near-daily basis to tens of thousands of audience members in every industry including banking, manufacturing, computer technology, transportation, government, medicine, law and public education. He makes his home outside of Toronto, Ontario with his amazing wife and son.

Visit cjcalvert.com

ENDNOTES

[i] https://www.who.int/docs/default-source/coronaviruse/situation-reports/20200121-sitrep-1-2019-ncov.pdf
[ii] **First fatalities on American soil of COVID-19.** https://www.cidrap.umn.edu/news-perspective/2020/04/coroner-first-us-covid-19-death-occurred-early-february
[iii] https://bc.ctvnews.ca/first-canadian-covid-19-death-recorded-in-b-c-health-officials-say-1.4845180
[iv] https://www.who.int/emergencies/diseases/novel-coronavirus-2019/events-as-they-happen
[v] https://ottawacitizen.com/news/local-news/coronavirus-doug-ford-tells-families-they-should-travel-and-enjoy-themselves-on-march-break
[vi] https://www.thestar.com/news/canada/2020/03/16/canadian-travellers-trying-to-return-trapped-by-border-closures-for-covid-19.html
[vii] https://globalnews.ca/news/6710672/canada-coronavirus-1000-cases/
[viii] https://www.forbes.com/sites/johnbbrandon/2020/05/12/this-is-huge-twitter-ceo-says-employees-can-work-from-home-forever/?sh=777248a84382
[ix] https://www.businessinsider.com/companies-asking-employees-to-work-from-home-due-to-coronavirus-2020#apple-ceo-tim-cook-said-that-it-seems-likely-that-most-employees-wont-be-back-in-the-office-before-june-2021-in-a-december-10-employee-town-hall-meeting-2
[x] https://www.businessinsider.com/bill-gates-business-travel-office-work-predictions-post-pandemic-2020-11
[xi] Parenting in the pandemic. https://www.usatoday.com/in-depth/news/education/2020/12/22/pandemic-parenting-how-covid-school-screens-stress-impacts-kids/6470288002/
[xii] https://www.weforum.org/agenda/2020/04/coronavirus-education-global-covid19-online-digital-learning/
[xiii] https://www.insidehighered.com/digital-learning/article/2020/10/27/long-term-online-learning-pandemic-may-impact-students-well
[xiv] https://www.nature.com/articles/s41598-020-78438-4

[xv] https://www.forbes.com/sites/tamarathiessen/2020/04/01/40-percent-less-flights-worlwide-air-travel-restrictions/?sh=7969216d6079
[xvi] https://www.washingtonpost.com/travel/2020/06/15/11-ways-pandemic-will-change-travel/
[xvii] https://www.travelandleisure.com/airlines-airports/air-new-zealand-trialing-vaccine-passport-app
[xviii] https://www.businessinsider.com/bill-gates-business-travel-office-work-predictions-post-pandemic-2020-11
[xix] https://en.wikipedia.org/wiki/Florence_Chadwick
[xx] Bridges, William. *Transitions*. 2004. Da Capo Press.
[xxi] Small area hypothesis. https://www.usatoday.com/story/life/health-wellness/2021/03/06/covid-19-pandemic-fatigue-ignoring-safety-measures-what-do/4579747001/
[xxii] https://www.theatlantic.com/health/archive/2021/03/what-pandemic-doing-our-brains/618221/
[xxiii] CAMH policy paper on mental health impact of COVID-19. https://www.camh.ca/-/media/files/pdfs---public-policy-submissions/covid-and-mh-policy-paper-pdf.pdf
[xxiv] SARS. https://www.cdc.gov/sars/about/faq.html
[xxv] https://www.ncbi.nlm.nih.gov/pmc/articles/PMC343855/
[xxvi] https://www.nejm.org/doi/full/10.1056/NEJMp2024046
[xxvii] https://www.mentalhealthcommission.ca/sites/default/files/2020-11/covid19_and_suicide_policy_brief_eng.pdf
[xxviii] Emotional Exhaustion During Times of Unrest. https://www.mayoclinichealthsystem.org/hometown-health/speaking-of-health/emotional-exhaustion-during-times-of-unrest
[xxix] https://www.ncbi.nlm.nih.gov/books/NBK279286/
[xxx] https://en.wikipedia.org/wiki/Maslach_Burnout_Inventory
[xxxi] https://edition.cnn.com/world/live-news/coronavirus-pandemic-vaccine-updates-01-20-21/h_66dd07ea9da21cee4edea1ea1757721f
[xxxii] https://www.medicalnewstoday.com/articles/i-have-never-seen-anything-like-it-says-new-york-city-doctor-about-covid-19#Isolating-from-family
[xxxiii] https://www.wbur.org/commonhealth/2020/05/11/health-worker-mental-health-coronavirus
[xxxiv] https://www.huffingtonpost.ca/entry/covid-19-burnout_ca_5f31b5d2c5b6fc009a5c1a6a
[xxxv] https://www.theglobeandmail.com/business/article-people-are-at-the-point-of-emotional-exhaustion-why-white-collar/

xxxvi https://www.camh.ca/en/health-info/mental-illness-and-addiction-index/depression
xxxvii **Logotherapy as a means to treat depression.** https://positivepsychology.com/viktor-frankl-logotherapy/
xxxviii Viktor Frankl, *Man's Search for Meaning* (New York, Simon & Shuster, Inc. 1984)
xxxix Stephen Covey. *The 7 Habits of Highly Effective People*. (New York. Fireside. 1990.)
xl **Our explanatory style**. Explanatory style, expectations, and depressive symptoms. Chrstiopher Peterson, Robert S. Vaidya. Science Direct. https://www.sciencedirect.com/science/article/abs/pii/S019188690000221X
xli **5 Things That Aggravate Anxiety.** https://calmer-you.com/5-things-aggravate-anxiety/
xlii **Is Being Hangry Really A Thing?** https://health.clevelandclinic.org/is-being-hangry-really-a-thing-or-just-an-excuse/
xliii **Pain Causes Anger. Can Relieving Anger Relieve Pain?** https://www.mcgill.ca/oss/article/health-news-you-asked/you-asked-pain-causes-anger-can-relieving-anger-relieve-pain
xliv **Cortisol — Its Role in Stress, Inflammation, and Indications for Diet Therapy.** https://www.todaysdietitian.com/newarchives/111609p38.shtml
xlv https://en.wikipedia.org/wiki/Hebbian_theory
xlvi https://psycnet.apa.org/record/1977-25733-001
xlvii Bryan Dyson. https://www.linkedin.com/pulse/5-balls-life-speech-coca-colas-former-ceo-olivier-chambe/
xlviii **To prevent an airplane stall, push the stick down.** https://aviation.stackexchange.com/questions/15575/is-a-pilots-instinctive-reaction-to-a-stall-counter-intutive
xlix https://www.mindful.org/
l https://www.moneysense.ca/save/debt/canadas-climbing-debt-to-income-ratio-what-you-need-to-know/
li Simple and Complex Carbohydrates. *CanFitPro Foundations of Professional Personal Training*. 2007. Human Kinetics, Windsor.
lii **Brown rice versus White Rice.** https://www.medicalnewstoday.com/articles/319797
liii **Apples as a good carbohydrate.** https://www.everydayhealth.com/diet-nutrition/diet/good-carbs-bad-

carbs/#:~:text=The%20three%20main%20types%20of,for%20you%20and%20what's%20not.
[liv] **Pancreas secrets insulin.**
https://www.medicalnewstoday.com/articles/316427
[lv] **Glucose stored as fat.** https://healthcare.utah.edu/the-scope/shows.php?shows=0_7frg4jjd
[lvi] Your blood is 90% water.
https://www.medicalnewstoday.com/articles/290814
[lvii] Effects of severe dehydration.
https://www.healthline.com/health/food-nutrition/why-is-water-important#antiaging
[lviii] **Water boosts metabolic rate.**
https://www.healthline.com/health/food-nutrition/why-is-water-important#immunity
[lix] **Water helps regulate mood.**
https://www.healthline.com/health/anxiety/dehydration-and-anxiety#hydration-and-anxiety
[lx] **Water decrease affects cognition.**
https://www.ncbi.nlm.nih.gov/pmc/articles/PMC6068860/
[lxi] **Water regulates body temperature.** https://sciencing.com/water-stabilize-temperature-4574008.html
[lxii] https://www.heartandstroke.ca/heart-disease/treatments/medications/diuretics
[lxiii] **Impact of sleep deprivation on cognition.**
https://www.healthline.com/health/sleep-deprivation/sleep-deprivation-stages#timeline
[lxiv] **Effects of sleep deprivation on short term memory.**
https://www.healthline.com/health/sleep-deprivation/effects-on-body
[lxv] **Sleep disorders affect 40 percent of Canadians.**
https://www.sciencedaily.com/releases/2011/09/110908104005.htm
[lxvi] https://www.news-medical.net/news/20201217/COVID-19-pandemic-affects-sleep-habits-leads-to-further-stress-and-anxiety.aspx#:~:text=The%20COVID%2D19%20pandemic%20is,further%20dependence%20on%20sleep%20medication.
[lxvii] https://www.nigms.nih.gov/education/fact-sheets/Pages/circadian-rhythms.aspx
[lxviii] https://www.ncbi.nlm.nih.gov/pmc/articles/PMC7375451/
[lxix] **Effects of Alcohol on REM and sleep.**
https://www.webmd.com/sleep-disorders/news/20130118/alcohol-sleep

[lxx] **Sleeping pills cause next-day drowsiness.**
https://www.helpguide.org/articles/sleep/sleeping-pills-and-natural-sleep-aids.htm
[lxxi] **Sleep pills inhibit GABA receptors in the brain.**
https://www.webmd.com/sleep-disorders/features/sleeping-pills-what-need-know
[lxxii] **Melatonin as a sleep supplement.**
https://www.hopkinsmedicine.org/health/wellness-and-prevention/melatonin-for-sleep-does-it-work
[lxxiii] **Chamomile tea effects on sleep.**
https://www.healthline.com/nutrition/5-benefits-of-chamomile-tea#TOC_TITLE_HDR_1
[lxxiv] **1 in 5 deaths caused by heart disease and stroke.**
https://www.conferenceboard.ca/hcp/provincial/health/heart.aspx
[lxxv] **2nd leading cause of death in Canada is heart disease.**
https://www.canada.ca/en/public-health/services/publications/diseases-conditions/heart-disease-canada.html
[lxxvi] Heath, Chip and Dan. *Switch*. 2010. Random House Canada. Toronto.
[lxxvii] **How we form habits, change existing ones.**
https://www.sciencedaily.com/releases/2014/08/140808111931.htm
[lxxviii] https://venturebeat.com/2020/04/02/zooms-daily-active-users-jumped-from-10-million-to-over-200-million-in-3-months/
[lxxix] https://tmb.apaopen.org/pub/nonverbal-overload/release/1
[lxxx] https://www.cbc.ca/news/technology/zoom-fatigue-is-setting-in-1.5585933
[lxxxi] https://www.psychiatrictimes.com/view/psychological-exploration-zoom-fatigue
[lxxxii] https://www.bbc.com/worklife/article/20200421-why-zoom-video-chats-are-so-exhausting
[lxxxiii] https://www.jobillico.com/blog/en/4-signs-you-have-zoom-fatigue-and-what-you-can-do-about-it/
[lxxxiv] Duhigg, Charles. *Smarter Faster Better*. 2016. Penguin Random House Canada
[lxxxv] http://en.wikipedia.org/wiki/Cortisone
[lxxxvi] https://www.nbcnews.com/healthmain/how-do-people-find-superhuman-strength-lift-cars-921457
[lxxxvii] https://www.ccsa.ca/sites/default/files/2020-04/CCSA-NANOS-Alcohol-Consumption-During-COVID-19-Report-2020-en.pdf